The Entrepreneur's IPO

The Insider's Roadmap to Taking Your Company Public

The Entrepreneur's IPO

The Insider's Roadmap to Taking Your Company Public

Peter Goldstein

ISBN-13:
979-8-9891711-0-1 Paperback
979-8-9891711-1-8 Hardcover
979-8-9891711-2-5 eBook
LCCN: 2023917542

Exchange Listing Publishing
Fort Lauderdale, Florida

www.exchangelistingllc.com

CONTENTS

DEDICATION

This book is dedicated to my children, Grace and Seth, who remain a driver for purpose in my life. My intention for this book is to be more than just a collection of words bound by pages.

It is my desire for it to serve as an embodiment of inspiration and a reminder that even in the darkest of hours, greatness can be conceived, and our authentic strength emerges, unwavering in the face of adversity.

Life is a profound journey which we are on together and is filled with peaks and valleys. I hope to share the wisdom that has come from enduring hardships, embracing determination and the transformative results of applying yourself.

As each of you embarks on your unique life paths, always remember that the combination of diligent work effort and steadfast values are the foundation bedrock upon which dreams are conceived and fully realized.

Know this: I stand as a steadfast supporter, cheering you on with unwavering devotion at every step along your extraordinary journey and I am always in your corner.

With all my love,
Dad

ACKNOWLEDGMENTS

First and foremost, I have immense appre- ciation to Gregg and Jill Jaclin for your unwavering faith in me and our enduring friendship and business collaboration spanning two decades. Your trust in me personally and in my leadership has been a cornerstone of our shared success, and your friendship has been a source of strength and a driver behind our collective achievements. Your unwavering support has been a constant source of motivation for me, whether it's during difficult times or celebration of our successes.

As I have grown as a man and a leader, I understand the significance of our trusted relationship, not just in our business partnership but also in our personal life. This trust has allowed us to collaborate effectively, navigate challenges, and seize opportunities together. Your confidence in my leadership approach has truly been a catalyst for our growth.

Looking back at our diverse experiences, I look forward to the enormous potential waiting to be unlocked as we journey further. Our shared adversities have fortified our union and imparted valuable resilience and wisdom, preparing us for future challenges. Our shared journey through hardships has strengthened our partnership and has also provided us with invaluable resilience and wisdom, which will undoubtedly be assets as we face new challenges ahead. Thank you for being not only my valued business partner but also a cherished friend. I deeply appreciate our partnership, and I hold our friendship in the highest esteem and with profound gratitude.

I want to express my gratitude and heartfelt thanks to all who have contributed to this book. Your expertise and dedication have greatly enriched the content and made this a more comprehensive, insightful, and valuable piece of work. Your expertise brought a unique perspective that added depth and authenticity to the book. Your contributions have undoubtedly elevated the quality of the content and made it more impactful and meaningful. Thank you for your generosity in sharing your time, expertise, and experiences, which has made a profound difference in the final outcome of the book.

I would also like to express my sincere gratitude to Shirley de Bruyn (Erasmus) for her unwavering support in the creation of this book. Her invaluable contributions, guidance, and dedication to this project have been instrumental in making it a reality. Thank you, Shirley, for your patience, friendship and being an essential part of this journey.

With special thanks to the following colleagues and friends
for their invaluable knowledge:

David Meltzer
Peter Tuchman
Dan McClory
Steve Yakubov
Benjamin Zucker
Brian Cavalli
Michael Cohen
Seth Farbman
Jonathan Rich
Richard Heft
Chris Mayo
Gary Herman
Luisa Ingargiola
Neil Reithinger
Zachary Blumenthal
Erik Sloan
Elliott Milian
Brian Zucker
Bill Caragol
Andrew Tucker
Ross Carmel
Jay Heller
Paul Dorfman
Marc Seelenfreund
Vlado Bosanac

FOREWORD

by
David Meltzer

David Meltzer is the co-founder of Sports 1 Marketing, and former CEO of the renowned Leigh Steinberg Sports & Entertainment Agency, which inspired the movie, Jerry Maguire. He is a three-time international best-selling author, Top 100 Business Coach, host of the top entrepreneur podcast, The Playbook, and Executive Producer of the Amazon television series, 2 Minute Drill. He is featured in many books, movies, and TV shows, such as World's Greatest Motivators, Think and Grow Rich: The Legacy, and Beyond the Secret, which is streamed on Netflix.

An Initial Public Offering (IPO) is a milestone that many entrepreneurs dream of. Indeed, in this fast-paced era, opportunities abound, but so do the obstacles that can make or break your venture. As an entrepreneur, understanding your timing and risk tolerance is paramount when it comes to making life-changing decisions for your business. Therefore, if you're planning to IPO your company, it is vital to understand the steps ahead of you. It's no accident that you have picked up this book.

I can assure you that it will streamline your approach to going public.

The Entrepreneur's IPO is written by a seasoned entrepreneur, Capital Market executive, and IPO advisor with decades of financial experience. This book is your ticket to unraveling the intricacies of pursuing a micro-cap or small-cap IPO. When applied with precision, Peter Goldstein's pragmatic insight and perspective have the power to transform the trajectory of your business.

An IPO can be a game-changer for any entrepreneur, regardless of their industry. Yet, the path to a successful IPO is laden with challenges that demand a deep understanding of the process.

Fear not, this invaluable guide will lead you step-by-step through the IPO journey with intellect, intuition, and, most importantly, unwavering confidence. Peter's background as a C-suite executive and his hands-on experience on Wall Street ensure that the strategies shared within these pages are not just theoretical but also practical and actionable.

What sets *The Entrepreneur's IPO* apart is its laser focus on the qualitative and quantitative elements crucial for engaging the right investment bankers, investors, industry experts, board members, and other team players.

This comprehensive resource not only equips you with the knowledge needed to take your company public but also provides insider perspectives that can mean the difference between surviving and thriving. Armed with the wisdom found in these pages, you'll effortlessly sidestep disastrous missteps and conquer daunting obstacles.

Timing and risk tolerance lie at the heart of any investment strategy. By meticulously assessing market conditions and understanding your own appetite for risk, you'll seize opportunities and make informed decisions. This book delves deep into these critical factors, thereby cultivating the foresight and acumen necessary for IPO success.

The Entrepreneur's IPO is a testament to the power of knowledge and experience. Peter's dedication to distilling his expertise into this comprehensive guide is admirable, as he seeks to empower entrepreneurs like you to fearlessly pursue their IPO dreams. May this book serve as your compass to guide you toward a prosperous future by navigating the exhilarating yet challenging waters of the IPO process.

So, strap in, prepare for the ride of a lifetime, and let *The Entrepreneur's IPO* unleash the boundless potential within you and your business.

Your journey of going public starts now.

PREFACE

As I sit down to write this preface, I am filled with a sense of gratitude and humility. I started this journey of writing my first book during the COVID-19 pandemic. I have long joked about writing a book about my adventures in the micro-cap and small-cap space and it is with great honor that I share my experiences, insights, and wisdom gained throughout my journey as a seasoned executive and entrepreneur in the ever-dynamic realm of Wall Street. Over the course of my career, spanning more than three decades, I have had the privilege of serving as a founder, C-suite executive, board member, and investor for both public and private companies.

As an expert in navigating the ever-changing climate of Wall Street, I've emerged as an international voice for the evolving micro-cap and small-cap industry. Additionally, I've successfully launched several highly innovative companies amidst today's disruption and shifting investment practices.

On my twenty-fourth birthday, I filed for my first business license at City Hall on Centre Street in Manhattan. I built that business from scratch with hard work, determination, and without outside capital or prior business experience. I followed my instincts and produced great results and my first exit was at the age of thirty. Since then, I have continued with my passion for entrepreneurship and working with others to build emerging growth companies. In 1999, I founded and became chairman and CEO of Grandview Capital Partners, Inc. (GCP), which is a specialized boutique investment bank that provides innovative financial services to select entrepreneurial emerging growth companies. I also serve as the founder, CEO, and managing director of Exchange Listing, LLC. (EL), which offers specialized advisory services in the strategic planning and implementation of an IPO and listing on a senior exchange, such as Nasdaq or NYSE, for private companies, or those listed on alternate exchanges. In addition, I have founded Emmis Capital, which is a specialized investment fund that provides growth capital to companies that are undertaking a public listing.

I have a master's degree in International Business from the University of Miami and an Advanced Corporate Director Certificate from Harvard Business School. I was a FINRA Registered Representative from 2007 to 2017. During this time, I held several securities licenses.

I am a member of the Forbes Finance Council. I regularly contribute to financial publications to share my wealth of knowledge in the micro-cap and small-cap sector.

These roles and experiences have not only provided me with invaluable business acumen but also granted me a front-row seat from which to witness the ebb and flow of the micro-cap and small-cap landscape.

I have learned that, in the world of finance (and life), change is constant and a perpetual dance, where the rhythm and demands of innovation set the stage for both triumph and tribulation. It is within this ever-changing climate that I have navigated these volatile waters and emerged as a voice of experience and expertise in the micro-cap and small-cap industry, both nationally and internationally.

As an industry expert, I have witnessed firsthand the transformative power of adaptability and resilience. I have honed my skills, developed a keen eye for choosing partners, projects, and emerging trends, and successfully launched several highly innovative companies. It is through these ventures that I have learned the art of balancing risk and reward, harnessing uncertainty as a catalyst for growth, and capitalizing on the opportunities that arise in times of change.

In the pages that follow, I aim to share the invaluable lessons I have learned. These lessons were forged from real-world experience on the front lines and trenches of Wall Street. This book is not just a reflection of my personal journey. Rather, it is a practical guidebook for aspiring executives and entrepreneurs who wish to thrive amidst today's disruption and shifting investment practices.

Within these chapters, you will find practical insights, strategic frameworks, and actionable advice that will empower you to navigate the complexities of Wall Street with confidence and poise. Whether you are an aspiring Capital Market executive seeking to ascend the public listing ladder or an entrepreneur looking to launch your first IPO, the information in this book comes largely from my years of experience as an entrepreneur (Capital Markets) and from leading many companies through IPOs as an independent advisor. After reading this book, you'll be able to effectively assess your company's IPO readiness, know exactly what steps to take, and in which order, as you embark on your IPO journey, and forge a path toward success that is uniquely your own.

I aim to continually support the innovation economy of entrepreneurial emerging growth companies worldwide that are uniquely positioned to access transformational growth capital and global capital markets and navigate them to IPO.

INTRODUCTION

Pursuing an Initial Public Offering (IPO) is something many entrepreneurs will only experience once. The journey to an IPO can be a long road. Functioning as a public company, while incredibly satisfying, demands attention to detail that many entrepreneurs are unprepared for. We've been made to believe that an IPO is reserved for the biggest, most popular companies only. But I'm here to tell you that simply isn't true. You *can* take your entrepreneurial growth company public and raise transformational capital from the public markets at an earlier stage than most people think is possible. I'm going to show you how. That is where this book comes in. Our aim is to provide a comprehensive guide for small-cap and micro-cap companies looking to IPO. We will cover everything from the basics of the IPO process to the complexities of financial reporting, regulatory compliance, and investor relations.

2021 was the biggest IPO year ever with extraordinary volumes globally. The global IPO market delivered 2,682 IPOs and raised 608 billion dollars. The largest IPO globally in 2021 was the 13.7 billion dollars IPO of Rivian Automotive on NASDAQ. During 2022, the market saw a dramatic decline in IPOs after a year of incredible IPO growth. Despite this, micro-cap and small-cap companies continued to dominate the 2022 IPO market in the US.

This book is designed to be a practical guide for entrepreneurs, executives, and investors who want to understand how to go public successfully. It is based on the collective knowledge and experience of industry experts who have been involved in numerous small-cap and micro-cap IPOs and have seen firsthand what works and what doesn't.

Whether you are a company founder looking to take your business to the next level, an investor seeking to understand the risks and rewards of small-cap and micro-cap IPOs, or a professional advisor helping clients navigate the IPO process, this book will provide you with the knowledge and insights you need to succeed.

I believe that going public can be a transformative event for small-cap and micro-cap companies, and I hope that this book will serve as a valuable resource for anyone looking to make the journey. At the end of each chapter, we have also invited industry experts to provide their tips and we are honored that they are willing to share their knowledge in this book.

So, what are micro-cap and small-cap companies?

A micro-cap company is a publicly traded company in the US with a market capitalization between approximately fifty million dollars and three hundred million dollars. Micro-cap and small-cap companies have greater market capitalization than nano-caps, and less than small-, mid-, large- and mega-cap corporations. Small-cap companies have a market value between three hundred million dollars and two billion dollars. As the name implies, a mid-cap company falls between large-cap (or big-cap) and small-cap companies.

What is a small-cap company?

A small-cap company has a market capitalization of three hundred million dollars to two billion dollars. These companies are appealing to investors because they have the potential for significant growth, that is, the potential to become large-cap stock companies (companies with a market capitalization of ten billion dollars and more).

Although small-cap and micro-cap company IPOs aren't regularly making the headlines, there has been a robust micro-cap and small-cap IPO market since 2019. We have also seen an increase in Special Purpose Acquisition Company (SPAC) deals. While they're not as appealing to some when they first come to market, SPACs increase the supply of smaller public companies.

In this book, I will take you through the process of preparing for a micro-cap and small-cap IPO from the perspective of someone who has helped a significant number of companies successfully IPO, even in a year that saw the most significant downturn in quite some time. With this book, you will have the knowledge and tools needed to prepare for an IPO well in advance, know what to expect from the IPO, and take your company public successfully.

Armed with the tools I will be providing, you'll have the opportunity to see your company name on the ticker, ring the opening or closing bell, and ultimately receive the investment and funding your business deserves. I've seen it happen repeatedly. My advice has been a catalyst for countless CEOs who went on to realize the goal to take their company public on the NASDAQ or the NYSE and achieve their entrepreneurial dreams.

CHAPTER 1
WHY YOU SHOULD CONSIDER AN ENTREPRENEUR'S IPO

You've probably heard about some of the bigger IPOs of the past few years, such as Johnson and Johnson's consumer-health spinoff, Kenvue (NYSE: KVUE), which went public in 2023, Corebridge Financial Inc. (NYSE: CRBG) in 2022, and online retailer Warby Parker (NYSE: WRBY) in 2021, and that each raised billions of dollars through IPOs. Many entrepreneurs are unaware that even early-stage, pre-revenue companies from around the globe can raise capital and list on US senior exchanges. Until recently, there was a belief that a company needed a minimum of one hundred million dollars in revenue to attract an underwriter to go public.

While small company IPOs do not often draw headlines, there has been a robust micro-cap and small-cap IPO market as more of these companies enter the public markets through standard IPOs. I firmly believe it is not the case that the biggest IPOs are the best IPOs.

In addition to a traditional IPO, there are alternative methods to go public, and perhaps you've also heard about SPACs, which is a buzzword on Wall Street. These companies are shell corporations listed on the stock exchange and formed to acquire a private company to bring it public without going through the traditional IPO process. The increase in SPACs, which has come to market, has also increased the supply of smaller public companies.

Today's robust markets present companies with several avenues to raise capital. Perhaps the most well-known and anticipated way to raise capital is indeed through the IPO process. As these traditional forms of funding capture the world's attention, the micro-cap or small-cap IPO often takes a back seat to higher visible deals partly because it is misunderstood and underappreciated. Micro-cap and small-cap companies are too small for large investment banks, fund managers are not sufficiently researched, and some have no analyst coverage. The lack of institutional following can lead to inefficient market pricing and an undervalued company.

The micro-cap and small-cap IPO, however, represents a great opportunity and a shift in the capital markets space, particularly for companies with a market capitalization between fifty million dollars and three hundred million dollars (i.e., micro-cap and small-cap). Therefore, I assert that a micro-cap or small-cap IPO is a unique funding opportunity for entrepreneurial companies to access capital and gain access to the public markets.

Many entrepreneurs are unaware that even early-stage, pre-revenue companies from around the globe can raise capital and list on US senior exchanges. Until recently, there was a belief that a company needed a minimum of one hundred million dollars in revenue to attract an underwriter to go public. Now, accepting the additional risk of liquidity and price volatility (particularly during periods of economic contraction because they are less prepared to deal with sharply declining demand than large-cap companies are) investors can access potentially high-growth companies directly, and entrepreneurs have a clear path into internationally recognized capital markets.

THE SHIFTING IPO MARKET

A development-stage or emerging-growth company listing on a senior exchange is a significant investment opportunity for a wide range of companies and investors. It also offers a chance for unmatched stock appreciation, added job creation, and economic stimulus as the company grows. Similarly, by listing on a senior exchange, a broader range of investors can invest in public companies and participate in their growth and wealth creation.

While everyone wants to invest in the next unicorn, these types of companies are mostly owned by large institutional shareholders, such as BlackRock, Vanguard Asset Management, Goldman Sachs, and J.P. Morgan, as well as private equity and venture capital investors. This limits the smaller retail investors, who might not have access to the same amounts of capital and opportunities to invest.

Unlike unicorns with more than one billion dollars in market value, micro-cap and small-cap companies can provide an excellent opportunity for entrepreneurs to reap the rewards of publicly listing their stocks and a significant benefit for early investors. This is especially true for smaller, high-growth companies in emerging industries, such as early-stage health care, technology, life science, electric vehicles, and financial services.

Capital markets are seeing a flow of public money, which means that investors are willing to risk investing in newer or early-stage companies, as they are betting that the company could become the next big thing. As a result, micro-cap and small-cap, publicly traded companies are going public sooner than they have ever been able to before. These are just a few of the potential advantages of micro-cap and small-cap IPOs:

- Create more capital-raising opportunities and financing options, typically at a higher valuation and a lower cost of capital.

- Establish a value for the company's securities and create a public market for them.

- Increase liquidity for existing and future investors and provide an exit strategy for venture and institutional investors.

- Increase legitimacy and visibility, which can, in turn, generate greater interest in and awareness of the company.

- Create a second currency with the company's common stock, thereby allowing the use of that equity instead of cash for acquisitions, and attracting and compensating management, employees, directors, and strategic partners.

- Give investors who want to get in early on the high-growth phase of a company access previously available exclusively to venture capitalists and private equity firms.

As the prerequisites to enter the stock market continue to change, knowing what micro-cap and small-cap IPOs are will provide both the investor and the entrepreneur an edge over others in the market.

WHY SOME ARE CONSIDERING MICRO-CAP AND SMALL-CAP IPOS

I believe an IPO is a superior liquidity strategy that allows companies the option to raise additional capital by selling shares to the public. It provides capital to expand the business, fund research and development, or pay off debt. Other avenues for raising capital, via venture capitalists, private investors, or bank loans, may be too expensive. However, in my experience, these other avenues for raising capital are better options than selling or merging your company. Value destruction, poor communication and integration, and cultural differences are some of the most common reasons for unsuccessful mergers or acquisitions.

When you sell a company or turn over the reins to a venture capitalist investment, you're handing over the control of your company to someone whose primary interest is a return on investment. You may watch as the acquiring entity changes what you built and ultimately destroys everything you worked so hard to create. In contrast, an IPO allows you to retain management control of your company, and continue to choose how you want to manage it every step of the way. Listing on the NASDAQ stock exchange is an excellent opportunity for entrepreneurial growth companies to access capital and enter capital markets with a micro-cap and small-cap IPO.

Taking your company public is more accessible than ever. It is a valuable and essential vehicle to access growth capital and human resources. There's been a return to the high volume of IPOs seen during the dot-com era of the 1990s. However, after the dotcom bust, the Wall Street myth that small IPOs are too expensive and risky became widely accepted. During the dotcom bust, the notion that a small company should not take on the risk or burden of the costs, obligations and potential liability of an IPO became commonplace. This myth, which was perpetuated over the years, has created a barrier to entry at a considerable cost to entrepreneurs, investors, and the world.

Here's the good news: an IPO is perhaps more within reach than you might imagine, and it could be a significant way for your company to grow, access capital, and gain market share.

Tips from the Pros

Peter Tuchman, NYSE Floor Trader and Moderator at Wall Street Global Trading Academy

- *People should know that my perspective is from boots on the ground, watching the IPO's happen from the inside.*

- *I like to say an IPO is like building a house. Before you go public you exist behind a curtain, you may be the only one who really knows your business, but the IPO process is opening your house door and inviting everyone in so that people can see what's going on in "public" in all the nooks and crannies.*

- *An IPO is an excellent opportunity for global validation and exposure for your company. Once people know and understand who you are, they can become your customers, partners, and shareholders.*

- *The IPO process is your chance to tell your Company story and provide significantly enhanced visibility and access to capital.*

- *Something people don't always realize is that the way the stock opens is the way it will likely trade for the rest of its life, think of it this way; if you have a shabby building with weak materials it will tumble. If you build a strong structure, you'll have a strong foundation that you can continue to build on as a public company with long-term sources of funding.*

Dan McClory, Managing Director, Head of Equity Capital Markets, Head of China at Boustead Securities

- *For any company, an IPO can seem to be a far-off dream. But at Boustead Securities, we like to talk to companies and clients about the 'Permission to Dream' and we preach the 'Art of the Possible'. An IPO is possible for growth companies with the right team.*

- *So, why would you want to consider an IPO? An IPO can offer the least diluted form of capital and the chance to use shares to entice and use as currency. In addition, there is the prestige of being listed on a stock exchange.*

- *Finally, going public establishes a market value for the company, determined by investor demand and public trading. This valuation can be used as a benchmark for future financing activities, such as secondary offerings, follow-on offerings, or debt issuances. It provides a transparent market-based valuation that can be useful for attracting additional capital in the future.*

CHAPTER 1 SUMMARY

- You're probably used to hearing about massive IPOs that attract attention and hype in the media. However, you don't hear about an underappreciated and available exit strategy for micro-cap and small-cap companies.

- Micro-cap and small-cap IPOs are available to micro-cap and small-cap companies. They help create capital, investor opportunities, increased liquidity, legitimacy, and visibility.

- Taking your micro-cap or small-cap company public allows you to stay in control of the reins, as opposed to handing over control to a venture capitalist whose primary goal is a return on investment.

- A micro-cap or small-cap IPO is probably more available than you have considered.

CHAPTER 2
LET THE GAMES BEGIN!

Preparation for a micro-cap or small-cap IPO needs to begin well before the IPO date. Ideally, a company should start assessment anywhere from eighteen to twenty-four months before the actual IPO date. Going public is gratifying, but it requires significant internal and external resources. In addition, the complexities, cross-functional participation, and interdependencies of going public require effective management and a clear understanding of the content and process. Therefore, preparation and groundwork are critical to a smooth execution process.

The assessment process, which is arguably often underappreciated, is critical to positioning a company for going public. Therefore, starting and understanding the assessment process as early as possible, and implementing it in parallel with assembling the team and resources required in this process, are essential for a successful launch.

ARE YOU READY?

A company's business model determines how it should be run and presented to investors. It can be vital to build your business model with clear assumptions and milestones, then use those metrics to measure your company's progress. For those who are thinking about going public, there is a need to assess your business model. Know where your company is today, and get some clarity on where you need to be in one, three, or five years to drive the vision and valuation of your company in a public market.

As part of the assessment process, some of the most critical people will be those who can carry out the ongoing changes and improvements of the business. These people will usually be the Chief Executive Officer, the Chief Financial Officer, the chairman of the audit committee, and the auditor. Usually, the operating numbers and projections flow through them, so they will often be the first to identify any issues emerging across the company.

It's crucial to develop a strategy to anticipate current revenue growth. During the assessment process, figure out the transition timing for key roles and have these transitions occur pre-IPO so the changes are implemented before that critical time. For example, it is essential to hire an independent audit committee chair that meets the US Securities and Exchange Commission's (SEC) definition of a "financial expert." A strong and effective audit committee and chairperson will expedite working with the many corporate advisors involved in the IPO process, such as auditors, investment bankers, and external lawyers. In addition, they will boost the offering's credibility with investors.

THE ASSESSMENT PROCESS

It's important to understand that you cannot run a business if you do not know where you are headed. And you cannot resource your business correctly unless you know how it is performing. One of the ways to understand how your company is performing is to compare it to a peer group. Carefully select several peer group companies and evaluate your company's performance according to those competitors. Some of the areas to focus on include:

- Demonstrate to investors how you are performing against your peers where investors are concerned.

- Understand how the market will value your company and the measures it will use, including revenue, net income earnings before interest, taxes, depreciation, and amortization (EBITDA) or any other metrics.

- Look to cash-flow growth as a valuation metric regardless of your business, either Free Cash Flow (FCF), including capital and spending, or Operating Cash Flow (OCF).

- Assess the quality of the company's employees and professionals to build for the future.

A critical part of this process is putting the IPO team in place. This team will bear the brunt of the work of preparing the company to go public and keep the process going post-IPO. The CFO is a key member of a company going public. This person needs to understand the capabilities of the finance and legal team, and hire team members who will help to grow the business. In addition, finance members need a technical understanding of accounting, internal controls, and a solid fundamental knowledge of accounting principles.

You also want to include a SEC reporting specialist who understands the SEC guidelines and generally accepted accounting principles requirements. This person can comfortably communicate with management, auditors, and the board of directors.

PREPARING FOR FUTURE GROWTH

The assessment phase aims to get as complete a picture of the company and the supporting professionals you will depend upon as you start down the IPO path as possible. Identify as early as possible the weaknesses and systemic problems that will need to be addressed over the next twelve to twenty-four months, for example, incorrect or incomplete financial reporting and the accuracy of corporate annual reports (10K). These include audited financial statements and reports that are due quarterly as well as unaudited financial statements (10Q). Also, weaknesses in internal controls often fall lower on the list of priorities when preparing for an IPO because CFOs are focused on the bankers, financial statements, projections, appointing lawyers, and countless other pre-IPO tasks.

Assess the current state of the company's information systems, and what it will cost to bring those systems up to public company grade and run the business through the coming years of growth adequately. Determine whether system upgrades and implementation are needed to provide data and enterprise resource planning systems for development and scaling.

In preparing to go public, you must share the current and future of your systems with management and the board as well as get buy-in for implementation company-wide. Then, as changes begin to occur, assess the company's culture, and determine whether the executive team and board of directors have the mindset to grow, change, and adapt to being public.

DIG DEEP

Do your due diligence during the assessment and take the time to understand your company's issues, including pending liabilities, C-suite and board of director backgrounds, and human resources and employee issues. Then, work on developing and implementing solutions to address the potential problems.

Assess the current auditors to establish whether or not they are qualified to provide reports under public company guidelines. Be aware that any material weakness or significant deficiency will impact the company's valuation and disclosure requirements. It is crucial to determine what it will take to make your company compliant with the Sarbanes-Oxley Act of 2002 (SOX) and create a plan to fix roadblocks to regulatory approval. It is vital that you take your time with this. On average, it can take over a year to sort everything out.

TOO MUCH?

Don't worry if this sounds like too much to absorb and process. One of the easiest ways to prepare for an IPO is to hire a capital market adviser who can help you with the following:

- **Listing Strategy**: Develop a listing strategy with key stakeholders, the executive management team, and the board of directors. Once a clearly defined strategy is in place, all those involved will manage the process and provide enhanced transparency and accountability.

- **Corporate Governance**: As you move forward with the public listing, you must develop an independent board and committees. A capital market adviser can assist you in setting up this board and committees, and work with you on corporate charters that are acceptable to the NASDAQ Stock Market.

- **Capital Market Resources**: Introduce the company to the best class of service providers, including investment bankers, investor relations firms, legal counsel, accounting, auditing, transfer agent, and Edgar agent to deploy solutions more effectively and use your internal resources adequately.

- **Project Management**: Ongoing project monitoring and management throughout the public listing process is essential. As key milestones are hit, and the timeline progresses, a capital market adviser manages the working group, including your investment banker, attorneys, and auditors, to streamline the IPO process. This includes weekly calls or meetings as well as management of the S-1 Registration Statement filing and comment process.

Creating an achievable IPO plan for completion is vital. Commencing the execution as a private company will help you stay on track and meet key IPO objectives. These include maximizing IPO price and attracting a high-quality investor base.

Tips from the Pros

Steve Yukabov, CEO of Edgar Agents LLC

Determining the right time for an IPO depends on a combination of internal and external factors. While financial readiness and market conditions are critical, it's also important to consider factors like industry dynamics, competitive landscape, and the company's strategic goals. Engaging with financial advisors and underwriters can provide valuable guidance in assessing the timing and market conditions. I would also recommend the following:

- *Assess the management team's experience, expertise, and ability to execute the company's strategy. Investors will evaluate the leadership's track record, industry knowledge, and ability to adapt to the demands of being a public company. Robust corporate governance practices and a strong board of directors are also important for public company compliance.*

- *Going public entails complying with a range of regulatory obligations, including financial reporting, disclosure, and corporate governance requirements. It's essential to assess whether the company has the necessary systems, processes, and internal controls in place to meet these obligations. Seeking guidance from legal and financial experts is highly advisable.*

- *Going public means increased scrutiny from regulators, investors, analysts, and the media. The company's leadership should be prepared to operate in a more transparent and accountable manner. It involves providing regular financial disclosures, holding earnings calls, and responding to investor inquiries. Assessing the company's ability to manage increased public scrutiny is essential.*

Benjamin Zucker, Managing Director at Spartan Capital Securities

- *Your company should have a clear underlying business. You want a story that can be easily conveyed to (and understood by) retail investors and generalists.*

- *Your company should have a growing a financial profile. It is much easier to get prospective investors excited about the company when there are positive historical growth trends (in revenue, EBITDA, cash flow, etc.), especially since companies cannot show forward projections or give guidance when going public.*

- *You should find a CFO with public company experience. Being public comes with a host of regulations and requirements. Having an experienced public company CFO is a great way to make sure your company is prepared for the journey ahead.*

- *As for when to IPO, you want the market backdrop to be accommodating. But if the business will need significant cash, and private capital is tough to come by, then the public markets might provide additional opportunities or structures.*

CHAPTER 2 SUMMARY

- You should start preparing to go public anywhere between eighteen to twenty-four months before you plan to go public.

- Start by assessing how ready your company is to go public. Then, look at the business model and determine the steps needed in the next three to five years to prepare for going public.

- Start getting the CFO, audit committee, and auditor in place in preparation for your IPO and select peer-group companies to evaluate your progress against.

- Assess your financial reporting and internal systems. Do they need to be upgraded?

- If it all sounds like a bit too much for one person to handle, find an experienced capital market advisor that can help your company develop an achievable IPO plan.

CHAPTER 3
PUTTING THE
PUZZLE TOGETHER

For both new and experienced micro-cap and small-cap officers and directors, embarking on an IPO can be somewhat intimidating, especially since there are no virtual check-the-box micro-cap and small-cap IPO strategy guidelines that you can follow. Developing a comprehensive strategy is different for each company, but it is necessary to ensure a smooth IPO execution. Proper preparation is one of the key elements for the commencement of life as a public company, which can be a memorable and incredibly rewarding experience.

A micro-cap or small-cap company may consider an initial public offering as a growth strategy for various reasons. Whether it be financing expansion, an exit strategy, or recapitalizing, an IPO may be a very effective long-term strategy for early-stage micro-cap and small-cap companies. However, the journey to execute an effective IPO requires a strategic roadmap.

This involves detailed planning, clear and reasonable expectations, an appreciation of the unpredictable nature of the stock market, and an unwavering commitment to the result of becoming a successful publicly listed company. Developing an IPO roadmap requires that management construct a business model, systems, and processes that it can support and have investors believe in for a successful outcome. It will contain the key ingredients of an action plan, timeline, budget, communications, and team structure, including but not limited to the following organizational topics:

Listing Requirements: the necessary quantitative and qualitative requirements, along with the preparation and submission of listing applications and related documentation

General & Strategic: the company's operating philosophy and business model, including growth strategies and objectives for each business line

Finance: historical and projected financial results, including discussion of operating performance, revenue, operating expenses, EBITDA, net income, and earnings per share

Management or Board of Directors: the company's management team and employees, including any pending or anticipated changes to key management, board composition, governance structures, and/or corporate structure

Legal, Regulatory, and Risk Management: material disputes, litigation, claims or possible claims in existence, pending or threatened against the company

Corporate Communication: corporate communications, awareness strategy, asset development, guidelines, and communication policies

Environmental: appropriate licenses, permits, and approvals compliant in all material respects, and policies to ensure highest standards of health, safety, and quality

PIECE BY PIECE

Think of these initial steps as throwing all the puzzle pieces out of a box, laying them out in front of you facing the right way up, and then starting to put them all together. The roadmap is the picture on the front of the puzzle box (that is, Bell Ringing Day) and the steps ahead are the process of putting the puzzle pieces together. The IPO process and preparations thereof are complex and consist of multiple steps and documentation.

Prior to the IPO, the company must collect and deploy data and documentation that are required to go public. These data and documents will be closely scrutinized by third parties, such as investors, investment bankers, lawyers, the exchange, the SEC, and others. You'll need information relating to company finances, business plans, as well as responses to information requests from lawyers, investment bankers, the auditors, and the exchange. To make sure you are keeping track of this documentation, and are providing consistency and efficiency in this process, consider compiling a cloud-based digital data storage for the IPO.

Best practices would include an administrative person dedicated to this process as a single communication point who is responsible for the collection and organization of consistent financial and non-financial data.

ASSEMBLE THE PRE-IPO TEAM

Embarking on a micro-cap or small-cap IPO is a major step in the overall development of a company, and it will require a team with expertise and specialized knowledge. Before embarking on the IPO journey, assembling this knowledgeable IPO team will be crucial for your success. It can take longer than you might think to find the perfect members who will send a strong signal to the market about the strength of the company's leadership and governance. Indeed, the road to an IPO is challenging, but the right team can help firms find the best partners and the best opportunities.

Tips from the Pros

Brian Cavalli, Director of Sales at EdgarAgents

- *Developing a successful IPO strategy requires careful planning and a dedicated team. Here are key considerations and the ideal composition of an IPO team:*

- *Clear IPO Strategy: Begin by defining your objectives and timelines. Craft a comprehensive roadmap that outlines the steps from pre-IPO preparations to post-listing activities. Align your strategy with market conditions, investor expectations, and your company's growth plans.*

- *Cross-Functional Expertise: Assemble a well-rounded IPO team with individuals who bring diverse skills and knowledge. Key members may include:*

- *C-Suite Executives: Your CEO, CFO, and other top executives should lead the IPO efforts, providing strategic direction and overseeing the process.*

- *Legal Counsel: Engage experienced securities lawyers to ensure compliance with regulatory requirements, manage legal complexities, and guide you through the IPO process.*

- *Investment Bankers: Collaborate with reputable investment banks to act as underwriters and help structure the offering. They bring valuable market insights, investor connections, and deal execution expertise.*

- *Financial Advisors: Employ experienced financial advisors or accounting firms to assist with financial due diligence, audit preparation, and compliance with accounting standards.*

- *Investor Relations: Assign a team member to handle investor relations, communications, and building relationships with potential investors before and after the IPO.*

- *Internal Stakeholders: Involve key department heads, such as operations, HR, and IT, to ensure smooth coordination and alignment of internal processes with the IPO plan.*

- *External Specialists: Depending on your specific needs, consider engaging external specialists such as IPO consultants, PR agencies, and investor relations firms. They can provide additional expertise, support, and guidance throughout the IPO journey.*

Remember, a well-executed IPO strategy requires collaboration, coordination, and adherence to regulatory requirements. By assembling a capable and diverse IPO team, you can navigate the complexities of the process and maximize your chances of a successful public offering.

Michael Cohen, Partner at Marcum LLP

Here are some suggestions for an IPO roadmap:

- *Hire competent professionals that have sufficient previous experience.*

- *Set up a kick-off meeting in which a timeline and a plan are laid out. Schedule regular update meetings after that initial meeting to keep everyone on track and on schedule. During the initial meeting, the client (who often is not familiar with the entirety of the process) can also be in the loop and address complications. This is also where a little reality can be shared. The audit won't be completed in two weeks, the SEC won't clear the S-1 on the first draft, and the deal won't close in one month, so regular update meetings might help reduce the stress from fire drills.*

- *I think that companies need some walkaway point, which is the point at which they're not raising enough money for the IPO to make sense to them. I try to describe it as debt, where the ongoing costs of being a public entity are the interest. For example, if a company pays its auditors two hundred thousand dollars, its lawyers one hundred and twenty thousand dollars, and its financial consultants eighty thousand dollars, it has four hundred thousand dollars of ongoing annual expenses to be a public company. If that company raises five million dollars, that's equivalent to annual interest on that money of eight percent. Now, there are clearly other factors to consider, like the ability to raise more money, to use stock as currency in an acquisition, etc. But my point is that most clients don't adequately consider the future costs as part of the deal.*

- *Another pitfall I've seen companies fall into is when a commitment of fifty million dollars converts to a best effort. Inevitably, the actual raise is more like fifteen million dollars, which isn't enough to actually execute the business plan, and much of the money (and time) is spent trying to raise the next tranche. This goes to finding the right professionals in the right space that will offer good honest feedback.*

CHAPTER 3 SUMMARY

- It will be essential to develop a strategic roadmap for your IPO to ensure a smooth transition to public company.

- Developing an IPO roadmap will require the management team to construct a business model, systems, and processes that it can support and have investors believe in for a successful outcome.

- The IPO roadmap will contain the key ingredients of an action plan, timeline, budget, communications, and team structure. There are multiple steps involved in preparing for an IPO. Creating a roadmap allows you to see all the various parts and how they function together.

- You will need to keep track of a great deal of data and information in a dedicated cloud-based file that will be examined by investment bankers, auditors, lawyers, and the SEC.

- It will help to include an administrative person dedicated to this process as a single communication point responsible for collecting and organizing consistent financial and non-financial data.

- A pre-IPO team with expertise and specialized knowledge will help to ensure a successful IPO.

CHAPTER 4
ASSEMBLING THE DREAM TEAM

For private companies that are planning a micro-cap or small-cap IPO, a strong executive team and a board of directors are critical. A well-positioned team will increase the value of the company and provide confidence to potential investors.

One of the most important aspects of IPO readiness is a thorough assessment of the strengths and weaknesses of the current executive, founding team members, and employees.

It's best to start with the people because you will need the right people in the right positions to make decisions about what systems need to be put in place, how those systems will be set up, and how they will be managed pre-IPO.

The right combination of skills, experience, and different ways of thinking will be needed. So, it is crucial to understand the role each person plays. Teams do not operate effectively when they try to cover a shortfall in personnel or leadership. Leaving a key role or area uncovered will show up in the company's performance going forward.

COMPANY CULTURE

The pre-IPO stage of building a team is a unique opportunity to further shape the company's culture and to develop what a strong team for the company's growth would look like. Hiring for cultural fit is a critical factor to consider, given that company success can be fueled by attracting and hiring candidates who fit the personality of the company and are willing to share knowledge and ideas.

When hiring, you need to give priority to those people who will fit your company's culture and adapt best practices they've learned elsewhere to your company's culture. As you build a team, you also need to encourage new people to think differently about their roles and their contributions to the company's culture. Look not only for the basic breadth of knowledge, technical skills, and demonstrated problem-solving skills but also for great interpersonal skills.

Those you are hiring for the IPO team will consist largely of people from other areas within your company. Now you're going to task them with additional responsibility of being a part of the IPO team. There will also be other key hires from outside your company and independent professionals.

THE BOARD MEMBERS

When choosing board members pre-IPO, it will be beneficial to take the time to selectively choose substantive members who can help shape the board for success. Look for board members who have relevant financing expertise. While experience in a large-cap company can seem attractive, it may not translate into smaller company expertise. Individuals with knowledge of micro-cap to mid-cap financing are vital when the company is looking for new or additional funding.

You will also want to ensure the board members have an industry track record. Consider each board member's experience. Is it relevant to your industry? It is vital to have board members, especially for micro-cap to mid-cap companies, who can leverage their prior industry experience and provide counsel to emerging-growth firms.

The board members should have experience in public companies and corporate governance. Selecting board members who have a performance history with other public companies, or experience with ESG policies, can be incredibly helpful.

Finally, consider fully supportive board members. Look for those who share a personal belief in your company's business model and management team.

THE FINANCE TEAM

Establishing a solid finance team and accounting practices will be essential to your success as a public company. In most early-stage companies, the finance team typically has been hired to focus on basic bookkeeping.

However, as you prepare for the IPO, you likely will need to build your finance team to transition to a public company and meet the increased demands of SEC reporting requirements. You will need to look at building the processes and systems necessary for scale.

Unfortunately, and too often, rebuilding your finance team is not a simple matter of replacing old employees. Rather, it requires a variety of skills to sort out past accounting issues and set the stage to meet SEC financial reporting requirements.

OVERLOOKED HIRES – PRE-IPO MARKETING

Your marketing department must evolve with your business as it becomes public. This requires a different type of marketing talent to communicate your story to the financial community. Developing and maintaining a persuasive and compelling equity growth story, as well as your management team's credibility, is a unique skill. It typically goes beyond traditional marketing.

The marketing department's task is to communicate these changes to the marketplace in a consistent, timely, and thoughtful manner. Change, adaptation, and evolution are key to maintaining a constant assessment of your company's awareness in the market, positioning, and brand building. High-quality pre-IPO marketing is a critical phase in the IPO process. It's possibly the most exhausting phase for the management team.

LEGAL

An in-house General Counsel (GC) can be a great value-added hire to help lead the way through the SEC filings and all the new agreements that come with going public.

Having the right GC on the executive team, who has SEC knowledge, understands contract law, and is an excellent negotiator, can save time and reassure key stakeholders and investors.

RECRUITING

One of the great benefits of an IPO is that it can provide liquidity for the company's employees, which can be utilized in recruiting key employees to work for a company before it goes public. As a company grows, it will require new skills and different experience from all its employees. Therefore, it should not be surprising that a company will undergo turnover at various levels.

You can mitigate the damage of a bad hire by continually looking for and recruiting better people, either inside or outside the company. If your business is always growing, you will always be hiring. Start developing recruiting processes early, and identify specialized recruiters who can assist your efforts.

FIND THE DREAM TEAM

Put together your dream team rather than a team you need to force-fit. The IPO process requires a well-oiled machine, and this will require a team of individuals who can work together for the success of the company. Ultimately, the changes the company will be going through can be significant, and so it will need a strong, knowledgeable team to guide the process.

Tips from the Pros

Seth Farbman, Cofounder and Chairman at VStock Transfers

- *Surround yourself with a team that has been through the IPO process several times and that has worked together on prior deals.*

- *Most CEOs are well versed in the terms of their business, but it is worth the effort to become well versed in the IPO terms as well as how the shares move through the transfer system.*

Don't think that the day you start to trade on the exchange, you can put out a press release and sit back and watch the liquidity roll in. It is a multi-prong effort of services, day in and out.

Jonathan Rich, CEO of Sophia Advisors

- *Affiliate and align yourself with the best people you can, that is, people who have deep and complementary knowledge and strengths, are accessible and reliable, but also willing to challenge norms and opinions. Oftentimes, management teams default to people they know or feel most comfortable with and will agree with them and their choices. Building an echo chamber of groupthink is an awful place to be when trying to consistently iterate, broaden perspectives, and develop best practices.*

- *Bring friction and competition to a process. It sounds simple but, too often, management teams rely solely on people they know already, a recommendation from a trusted friend, investor, or perhaps board member, or even one service provider recommending a fellow provider they have worked alongside previously and successfully. While that's a good start, speaking to multiple groups of all types of providers, whether accounting, legal, insurance, transfer agents, or banking, is imperative in order to firmly understand the strengths, competencies, approaches, costs, personalities, and contrasts of each respective group. Having groups actively compete for your business allows management teams to make fully informed decisions and discharge their duties in the process by having objectively evaluated alternatives.*

- *In terms of accounting and legal teams, align with the teams who proactively express interest in and knowledge about your specific stage, business, and the industry in which you participate. Professional service providers will easily be responsive and reactive. But are they proactively helping you identify issues, best practices, and solutions based on specific and comparable experiences they are having with you and other similarly situated clients? It's easy for a firm to say "we have a capital markets group and experience" or "a team of dedicated healthcare industry lawyers or accountants." But how does that apply to you and your needs? How does that help you develop the frameworks you will need? It's also important to set expectations upfront not only on costs but also on relationships and who will handle your account.*

- *When it comes to an IPO or any type of capital markets initiative, developing a detailed action plan upfront with steps, timelines, roles, responsibilities, and deliverables is key to ensuring that all participants are on the same page and that communication is uniform. It allows you to identify issues, stay on target and cost, and enable each party to understand expectations around their individual responsibilities and how and when they connect to the larger process.*

CHAPTER 4 SUMMARY

- A strong board of directors will be crucial for a micro-cap or small-cap company planning to IPO. You will need to thoroughly assess the strengths and weaknesses of the current executives, founding team members, and certain employees.

- When filling roles in the company pre-IPO, carefully consider the cultural fit of the candidates not only for their basic breadth of knowledge, technical skills, and demonstrated problem-solving skills but also for great interpersonal skills.

- When making board member hires pre-IPO, look for relevant experience. And remember that individuals with knowledge of micro-cap to mid-cap financing are vital when the company is looking for new or additional funding.

- The finance team will help your company transition to a public company, and meet the increased demands of SEC reporting requirements. In addition, you will need to look at building the processes and systems necessary for scale.

- Don't forget about the marketing department! Developing and maintaining a persuasive and compelling equity growth story, as well as your management team's credibility, is a unique skill. It typically goes beyond traditional marketing.

CHAPTER 5
POSITIONING YOUR COMPANY STORY

Your journey to a micro-cap or small-cap IPO will begin well in advance, often as early as twelve to eighteen months before the bell-ringing day. One of the many steps in getting ready for an IPO, which is often overlooked and misunderstood, is pre-IPO communication and awareness. A sound plan is driven by a communication and positioning approach that articulates a company's value proposition in a way that resonates with the investment community.

Management teams are typically trained to communicate to their buying audience. But they will need to learn how to communicate and leverage thought leadership, product innovation, and material business development while the company is private. This will raise awareness among key stakeholders and the capital markets community well in advance of an eventual IPO.

PRE-IPO MARKETING

High-quality pre-IPO marketing is a critical phase in the IPO process, and possibly the most exhausting phase for the management team. Getting the messaging just right requires dedication and incredible attention to detail. Pre-IPO marketing is focused on the company's equity story, the management team, and the development of usual and customary company communication and marketing practices.

Compliant pre-IPO marketing is focused on brand development. It will not contain any forward-looking statements, plans, or predictions about the company's value or performance within regulatory requirements. During the pre-marketing period, the company will also begin to collect investor data for retargeting efforts that will begin at the time of listing. Compliant communication includes creating a standard for announcing milestones, key events, mandatory public company communications, business developments, and successes.

THE INVESTOR OUTREACH PROGRAM

A strong investor outreach program will create investor awareness in preparation for the day the company becomes listed. Hopefully, it will also attract a pipeline of potential investors pre-listing. From an internal perspective, the investor outreach program will help to prepare the company's leadership team for the various communication requirements for the IPO. It will establish a protocol for best practices of communication for a public company.

The investor outreach program will also allow the company's management to gather contact information of interested investors and analysts for retargeting after the company has gone public. Finally, and most importantly, the investor outreach program will define and refine the company's investor-focused story as well as the ideal target investor.

PREPARATION & HIGH-LEVEL DOCUMENTATION

During the pre-IPO marketing period, the leadership team will meet to determine the current thinking on the company's purpose, equity story, go-to-market timeline, and the key differentiators. This has likely been done from the company's point of view. During this process, the company's purpose, equity story, and go-to-market timeline will be repositioned to address the investor's point of view.

The management team begins identifying the right tools for mapping all marketing efforts to create a high-level corporate purpose document and craft a Feeder Copy for marketing efforts. During this time, the company also begins to create an assessment and inventory of all marketing supporting assets (such as logos, images, and videos) as well as a shared folder where relevant parties can access these assets.

REGULATORY COMPLIANCE

Before the public filing of a registration statement, the company begins corporate marketing and starts to establish the customary and usual marketing efforts. They create company visibility with targeted investor communities by using digital marketing, influencers, publishing, social media, and email or text messaging campaigns. This will provide an opportunity to capture investor or analyst contact information for retargeting efforts later.

After the SEC Registration, the company continues its customary and usual marketing, which is focused on brand awareness and retargeting information. The company will also continue to fine-tune marketing efforts (channel and positioning).

POST-IPO

After the company has gone public through an IPO, it will want to pivot its marketing from generating awareness and seeking contacts to creating and seeking investors. This will require a tightly synced marketing strategy that has been outlined by an experienced Capital Market advisor and a specialized agency. The strategy will focus on the company's equity story and the overall opportunity available to both retail and institutional investors. It will also be a time to map out the company's needs, expectations and timelines to use in the timing and strategy for the marketing campaign.

POST-LISTING STRATEGY

At first, many newly public companies enjoy high share prices fueled by investors' interest in IPOs, and by press coverage. However, the initial euphoria will quickly fade unless the market's interest in the company is properly and carefully maintained after the IPO. This is when the process of retelling and fine-tuning your company's equity story begins. As a public company, it's important to continually cultivate potential investors as well as research and analyst coverage. Additionally, the company will want to attract the optimal mix of investors to maximize liquidity and valuation.

The strategizing does not stop after listing. It is important to continue to create plans and timelines for expectations, milestones, key events, and financing needs, which will be beneficial to the company when supported by robust internal review and marketing campaigns.

A great IPO advisory firm will help with these needs. Such a firm will also help with product development roadmap milestones, merger and acquisition activities, expected timing for additional funding needs, closure of significant clients, and an intellectual property roadmap. For a post-IPO marketing strategy to have maximum returns on investment, it is critical that the marketing activities include communicating the company's business accomplishments in a well-packaged way.

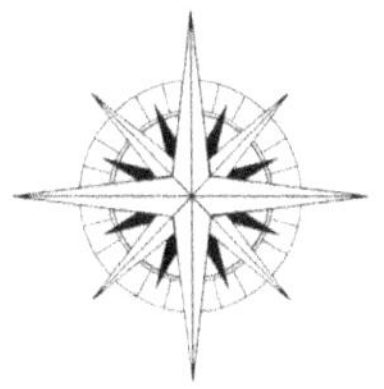

Tips from the Pros

Chris Mayo, Head of Primary Markets, Americas at London Stock Exchange Group

- *US private companies in the small and micro-cap space should also consider IPOs on overseas markets, like the London Stock Exchange.*

- *The London Stock Exchange has a strong track record of IPOs from smaller US private companies, quoted on its growth market AIM*

- *IPO transaction, ongoing listing costs, and litigation risk are far lower in London than on US exchanges*

- *With small and micro-cap IPOs making up a far higher proportion of IPO volume in the UK than in the US, high-quality brand name institutional capital is much more active in this space in the UK than in the US.*

- *Many small and micro-cap US companies have listed in London to support their growth and added a US exchange listing as they get larger*

- *The UK IPO process has more regulatory flexibility than the US. Testing the waters can be done much earlier with no regulatory input so companies can get a view of investor receptivity before investing more time and money into the IPO process. In addition, UK IPOs still have deal research, which leads to enhanced price discovery and more accurate price range setting and visibility on likely outcomes.*

- *The London Stock Exchange provides support to guide companies in understanding the listing requirements, process, costs, and how to pick the right team of advisors.*

- *Post listing, the London Stock Exchange's Issuer Services platform helps companies raise their visibility via a series of content management tools to highlight company branding, regulatory and company news, embedded social media feeds, equity research, company fundamentals, and upcoming events. Company capital markets-related events can be streamed via its SparkLive platform to reach millions of retail and institutional investors, including through Refinitiv Workspace.*

Richard Heft, President at Ext. Marketing Inc.

- **Know your audience.** *We all have a lot we want to say about our company's products or* services, but it's often better to approach your overall communications by thinking about what your prospective investors are looking for or interested in. Maintaining a strong, concise focus on your value proposition is always the best way to communicate to potential investors.

- **Make a plan ...** An investor-targeted campaign can include many facets and different methods of outreach. For example, running a paid media campaign on LinkedIn is likely to net a different outcome than purchasing ad space in a financial publication or distributing an email campaign to key contacts within your industry. It is a good idea to know where your potential investors get their information (i.e., social media, websites, newsletters, podcasts, email, etc.) and to explore the various strategies that might work best for your offering early on in any marketing campaign.

- **... but pivot when required.** Once you start marketing yourself to your target audience, review your metrics regularly to ensure people are seeing and engaging with your content. If you aren't getting the desired response to your communications efforts, it's worth testing a new message, creative, and/or platform(s), and then seeing if those adjustments help improve conversion. This process is called A/B testing, and it's a proven approach to achieving long-term campaign success.

- **Budget accordingly.** Although money is always tight when you are launching an IPO, it's important to ensure you continue communicating to potential – and existing – investors on an ongoing basis. This type of engagement will require an investment of capital that may initially seem difficult to commit to. That said, you do not want to miss the opportunity to generate momentum around your company when it is needed most.

- **Outsource to the experts.** The leadup to an IPO, and even the months and years afterwards, can be a whirlwind of tasks and responsibilities that often don't leave you with much time to market your business. Although most companies prefer not to add to their marketing headcount when there are so many competing priorities, it's important to continue positioning your company in the best-possible way with investors. There are a number of great outsourced marketing, investment relations and public relations service providers who can help you get the word out while you are focused on expanding your operations and preparing to go public.

CHAPTER 5 SUMMARY

- Pre-IPO marketing, communication, and awareness are vital. The management team will need to learn how to communicate and leverage thought leadership, product innovation, and material business developments.

- Pre-IPO marketing will focus on the company's equity story and brand development. It will not contain any forward-looking statements, plans, or predictions about the company's value or performance within regulatory requirements.

- Investor outreach will help the company's management gather contact information of interested investors and analysts for retargeting after the company has gone public.

- Before officially filing a registration statement, the company can start corporate marketing. First, the company's management will create company visibility with targeted investor communities by using digital marketing, influencers, publishing, social media, and email or text messaging campaigns.

- After the company has gone public through an IPO, it will want to pivot its marketing from generating awareness and seeking contacts to creating and seeking investors.

- As a public company, it's important to continually cultivate potential investors as well as research and analyst coverage. Additionally, the company will want to attract the optimal mix of investors to maximize liquidity and valuation.

- The strategizing does not stop after listing. It is important to continue to create plans and time-lines for expectations, milestones, key events, and financing needs.

CHAPTER 6
BUILDING THE BOARD

Based on what I've witnessed, suitable corporate governance can be one of the most difficult challenges companies face when preparing for a micro-cap or a small-cap IPO. It is a critical and necessary part of the IPO journey in order to operate as a compliant and sustainable public corporation. Governance requires processes, systems, and controls to ensure the effective and efficient use of resources for an organization to achieve its goals and objectives.

Some may notice that countless start-ups and entrepreneurial companies have operated and succeeded with limited governance. This is especially prevalent in a founder-led company. The transition to public company governance, and the new requirements that come with it, can be overwhelming for the management team. Implementing new procedures is time-consuming when reviews and approvals are required by outside parties, which can limit or slow entrepreneurial actions and cultures.

Is it possible to get the corporate governance up to speed well before becoming a public company? Yes, it is. Setting up public company governance and a board of directors should ideally begin about a year before the IPO date. Start by filling the two most important roles, namely, the audit and compensation committee chairs, because they are required to operate as a public company.

Each committee of the board has several procedures and processes to put in place. It's best to have these processes in place, while allowing the committees enough time to get settled in their roles, and begin holding regular meetings as soon as possible.

THE CORPORATE GOVERNANCE MINDSET

If done properly, good governance will improve the effectiveness, efficiency, and value of the company. However, implementing governance requires systems, controls, and the proper mindset. Overseeing governance and corporate culture is time consuming. Adapting to the mindset of being a well-governed public company requires a commitment from leadership.

This shift in mindset often includes incorporating systems for third parties to assess and review your company. For this reason, corporate governance certification practices should be in place well before the IPO date.

Good governance also requires the CEO to adopt several tangible processes for improved transparency. It's what good governance provides.

These processes include:

- Accounting and compliant financial reporting

- Information technology systems and processes

- Board operations and decision making

- Timely disclosure of material information in compliance with the SEC and exchange rules.

BOARD GOVERNANCE AND SELECTION

Selecting the best board members is crucial to the success of the company. They'll likely need specific skills and backgrounds to add serious value to the company. Large-cap expertise often doesn't translate exactly to the micro-cap ecosystem. Therefore, I recommend looking for those individuals who are best suited to your company. As a company approaches an IPO, it may also be beneficial to recruit one or more directors with public company experience. Engaged and value-added board members are what every shareholder, officer, and director will welcome. They also need to have the proper cultural fit and values that will set the tone at the top of the company. This, in turn, ensures proper governance throughout.

Board actions will include establishing ethical and operating standards, and encouraging a commitment from the rest of the board members and the executive leadership. For board members, these standards are the baseline for being recruited to the board, remaining on it, and being affiliated with the company.

Even CEOs who are highly attuned to corporate culture might have a limited understanding and experience of board governance. Among the attributes of proper board behavior is independence, experience, and skills, which will help the company determine who is eligible to serve as director on the board and to which committee each new director will be assigned. If they are properly implemented with the right people seated at the table, boards can be a competitive advantage for the CEO and an asset for shareholders.

ACCOUNTING AND FINANCIAL REPORTING

Good financial accounting and reporting processes are the foundation of proper governance. This includes metrics and reports for compliance as well as managing company performance. The process of implementing accounting, financial reporting, and governance must not be an afterthought. It needs to be part of the foundation of your company and it must start well before the IPO. This foundation starts with documenting each process in accounting, how account reconciliations occur, and who reviews them.

Putting these processes in place early in a rapidly growing company means preventing things from getting off track, which can occur very fast. The best approach to your IPO corporate governance is to set up the accounting and financial reporting from the beginning as if your company is already public. The sooner you get these processes in place, the more time everyone has to adapt to the change. Every company, private or public, must make annual filings. For public companies, filings are required quarterly and annually.

The SEC sets prescribed deadlines. Adapting to filing on a specific timeline could end up being a big learning curve and a challenge for micro-cap and small-cap companies. This is where good governance applies. With the right people, processes, and alignment among the team, these filings become better organized to be completed on time.

Having the right people to get accurate numbers promptly is the driver of the accounting and governance systems that you must set up internally. Finding the right external legal and audit support for compliance requirements, and ensuring proper review, will be a driving force of your company as a public entity.

You can implement strong corporate governance practices incrementally but know that it starts with the leadership team. The new board and each committee will create and regularly review the relevant charters, or Terms of Reference (TOR), and the board's policies. Carefully considered board governance is a key piece of corporate oversight in the micro-cap and small-cap sector. It is frequently an underappreciated part of the IPO process. But, when done thoughtfully, it will provide critical value to becoming a sustainable public company.

Tips from the Pros

Gary Herman, Managing Member at Galloway Capital Management

The role of the board of directors is crucial when a company is going public. The board plays a significant role in shaping the company's strategic direction, overseeing corporate governance, and ensuring compliance with legal and regulatory requirements. Here are some key aspects of the board's role during an IPO:

- *Board members must have the time to serve and a commitment to the long-term success of the Company. The board provides oversight of executive management throughout the IPO process and beyond. They assess the management team's capabilities, evaluate their readiness for the demands of being a public company, and ensure succession planning is in place, so the board members cannot be constantly changing.*

- *Board members should be able to add value based on their contacts and business experience. The board plays a role in investor relations efforts, especially during the IPO roadshow and beyond. They may participate in investor presentations, meetings, and conference calls to communicate the company's vision, strategy, and performance to potential and existing investors. The board helps build investor confidence, establishes credibility, and fosters positive relationships with shareholders so their contacts and business experience are crucial.*

- *Board members should have good judgment and be willing to make tough decisions when necessary for the good of the Company and its shareholders. The board oversees the identification, assessment, and mitigation of risks associated with the IPO. They work with management to identify potential risks that could impact the company's financial performance, reputation, or compliance. The board establishes risk management frameworks and ensures that appropriate controls and processes are in place to manage and mitigate those risks.*

Luisa Ingargiola, CFO at Avalon GloboCare & Board Director at Dragonfly Energy and Board Director at ElectraMeccanica

The importance of the board cannot be overstated during the IPO process. A strong and effective board inspires investor confidence, provides strategic guidance, and ensures sound corporate governance. They bring diverse perspectives, industry expertise, and experience to help navigate the complexities of going public. A well-functioning board can enhance the company's credibility, protect shareholder interests, and contribute to long-term value creation. In addition, the board offers the following:

- *The role of the Board is to provide governance and oversight to the management team and to set the corporate strategy which the management team is to execute.*

- *The Board should provide mentorship and guidance to the management team, especially in times of crisis which is why when selecting the Board, the founder should not just pick a group of their friends.*

- *Rather, board members should be selected based on specific areas of expertise (at least two with public company experience):*

  - Finance/Corporate Governance

  - Capital Markets

  - Sales/Marketing

  - Experience in areas specific to the company industry

CHAPTER 6 SUMMARY

- Selecting a suitable board can be one of the biggest challenges when preparing for a micro-cap or small-cap IPO.

- If done properly, good governance will improve the effectiveness, efficiency, and value of the company. However, implementing governance requires systems, controls, and the proper mindset.

- The CEO will need to adopt several tangible processes, including:

    ○ Accounting and compliant financial reporting
    ○ Information technology systems and processes
    ○ Board operations and decision-making
    ○ Timely disclosure of material information in compliance with the SEC and exchange rules.

- When selecting board members, don't be easily impressed by large-cap expertise. It doesn't always translate to the micro-cap and small-cap ecosystem.

- Instead, look for directors with public company experience.

- Proper financial accounting and reporting processes are the foundation of good governance. Put these processes in place early!

CHAPTER 7
FINDING A BANK YOU CAN BANK ON

A key component of the IPO process is finding the right investment bank and investment banking team within the micro-cap and small-cap community. For your company to go public, you need to establish relationships with a group of specialized financial institutions with expertise in the micro-cap and small-cap sector. You become part of this unique community when going public as a micro-cap or small-cap company.

SELECTING AN INVESTMENT BANK

Selecting the right investment bank and banker for you is critical to successfully structuring and executing your company's IPO. It is important to select an investment bank that focuses on micro-cap and small-cap investors. These are different from mid-cap or large-cap investors since market capitalization is more or less commensurate with a company's stage of business development. Investing in a micro-cap, small-cap, mid-cap, or large cap corresponds roughly to investors' risk and reward profiles.

Finding a bank that is the best fit for your company is not only about the size and sector in which you operate but also about the bank's history with transactions, experience, and client successes. Considering a bank's history with transactions, experience, and client successes will help you to identify the right individual banker. You want to choose your bank carefully. Similarly, make sure the lead banker is a person who will champion your IPO and provide the specific attention and resources you need.

Choose a lead banker that you can work with well, both in the present and in the future. The bankers must have a good rapport with management for the long term, including secondary offerings and capital market-related matters.

You should determine whether the lead underwriter will be the sole book runner. you should also find out who will be responsible for coordinating and leading a well-organized underwriting syndicate. Finally, you should ask your prospective bank about the banks it is likely to form a syndicate with, about its distribution capabilities, and about its distribution strategies.

Most companies will select several investment banks to lead the IPO, underwriting, and book running process. It's common practice for a company to invite several banks to compete for the rights to lead and manage that company's IPO. Ultimately, a company will select *one* investment banking firm as its lead underwriter to head up the process based on the firm's reputation, quality of research, and industry expertise. After choosing an IPO underwriter, the two parties will formally agree to terms through an underwriting agreement. This includes the amount of compensation the underwriter receives during the IPO.

THE INVESTMENT BANKING TEAM

Bankers for micro-cap and small-cap IPOs generally provide the same services. They work with many of the same buy-side institutions that invest in micro-cap and small-cap companies. They all have trading desks servicing buy-side institutions. And they are in the business of selling stock.

The investment banking team will help you navigate the process of going public and negotiating to sell your new stock offering to investors. Naturally, this is critical to getting the valuation right and setting the tone for your IPO. The investment bank you choose has a variety of purposes, including underwriting new stock issues, following up on debt and equity financings, overseeing mergers and acquisitions, and advising clients on strategic capital market matters.

The lead banker is an essential selection. This is the banking team member you will spend the most time with. This person will be an important asset to your team. Therefore, personality and fit are important for the success of a long-term relationship. As you'll discover, this person knows the market, that is, how the market is doing at any given moment. This person also has an understanding of the business and its strategy and the ability to position the company's story to get strong investor reception. This person will represent you to get you the best valuation and opening price.

When selecting the team, look at other IPOs the bankers have recently completed as well as the valuation and performance of those deals immediately after pricing. The team and the people who work in sales and trading are the ones who will be interfacing with investors. They need to believe in the company to be successful in selling the stock.

DO YOUR HOMEWORK

It is critical to do your homework before you get bankers involved. Compare relatively simple metrics such as:

- Revenue

- Revenue growth

- Sales and marketing as a percentage of revenue

- General and administrative (G&A) as a percentage of revenue

- Gross margins

- Operating margins

Understanding these metrics will change how you see and operate your business. These metrices will show how your business differs from your peer groups and help you identify areas of opportunity and improvement. Once you have done your homework, you are ready to talk to bankers. But do not rush the process.

Before engaging with bankers, you should have your historical and proforma financial model ready to present to bankers. In addition, you should articulate the financial assumptions that drive the growth of your business and where the company is headed in the future. These deliverables must be fleshed out before approaching and engaging bankers.

In addition, you'll want to understand the competitive landscape of comparable peer companies. It is important to compile a list of three to five private and public companies with which to compare your company.

This list will be based upon a similar business model or a common industry segment in which you compete. Next, look at these companies for comparable valuations and identify your similarities and differences with your peer group. Then, compare your business model to those benchmark companies and determine what makes your company unique. These metrics will be an essential and regular topic of discussion and analysis as you go through and beyond the IPO process.

ENGAGING THE BANKERS

Once you thoroughly understand your business and business model from a capital market perspective, it is time to engage the bankers. After you've identified banks, it's best to meet with as many as possible to gain different perspectives on your IPO. You can expect a long relationship with the bank and the research department. So, take your time to find the best fit.

Beyond the IPO, it is typical to have at least a one-year contractual relationship with the bank, including a fee tail, and right of first refusal. The goal here is to ensure that the sell-side research team truly understands your company's story, its history, where it's headed in the future, and its corporate culture. This part of the team needs to clearly understand these elements in order to effectively sell the company's story to potential bankers and investors. Begin this acclimation process as early as one year before the IPO.

PREPARING THE S-1 DRAFT

One way investment bankers can further add value is by assisting in preparing and writing the business section of the SEC registration. This section of the prospectus tells your company's story. It contributes to the content of the pitch deck used for your investor roadshow. This is known as the S-1 draft.

The work of preparing the S-1 draft properly can save significant time and a lot of frustration throughout the IPO process. Utilize the underwriter's experience with IPOs to review the S-1 and to get most of the registration done before selecting your bankers. The underwriter will also be instrumental in arriving at a valuation range of your company's offering as well as structuring your offering based on comparable companies, market intelligence, and the banker's expertise. Keep in mind that the value-add of the bankers' capital market team is that they understand how their customers will react to specific language and visuals. This will be a massive help in this part of the process.

There are many important considerations when selecting the right investment bank. Remember, the bank's reputation within the micro-cap and small-cap industry reflects on the company and needs to be factored into the decision.

As a final step, it is good practice to call a board meeting, present your case for the bank and banker you want to underwrite the IPO, and hold a vote to have the board involved in the selection.

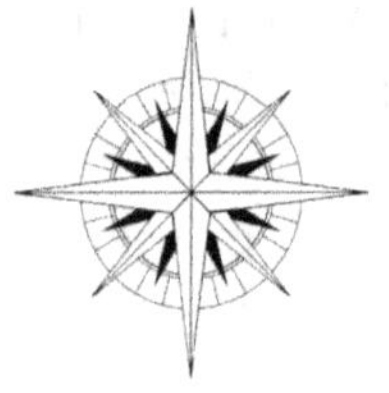

Tips from the Pros

Neil Reithinger, President Eventus Advisory Group, LLC

Finding a Suitable Investment Bank and Banking Team for an IPO:

- *Bank Selection: Choose a small-cap investment bank with a reputable and experienced banking team. Investigate their background, reputation, and track record as a team. Consider their reach in institutional, retail, and syndication areas.*

- *Market Awareness: Understand market trends and investor preferences. Investment bankers should be proactive and adaptable to changing market conditions. Stay informed to structure deals that cater to investor preferences.*

- *Leverage Data: Utilize IPO list reports and statistical data to evaluate the performance of potential investment banks. A track record of successful deals can be an indicator of future success, but new banks with experienced teams can also be viable options.*

- *Seek References: Reach out to references and CEOs of past IPO issuers to gain insights into how banks manage the IPO process. Assess their ability to navigate challenges and meet timelines.*

Preparing the S-1 Draft for an IPO:

- *Realistic Timeline: Develop a practical timeline that accommodates the SEC's comment periods, which each typically may take up to 30 days. Factor in potential multiple turns for the S-1 before clearing comments. Allow for at least 120 days for the SEC review process.*

- *Confidential Filing: Consider filing a Draft Registration Statement (DRS) confidentially with the SEC. This enables early review, helps to address initial comments, and provides time to finalize financials while staying ahead of financial statement staleness concerns.*

- *Continuous Updates: Maintain updated financials and disclosures at all times to prevent staleness and ensure transparency. Work closely with auditors to meet deadlines for annual audits and interim reviews.*

- *Ready to Go Live: When the DRS is substantially reviewed and comments are addressed, finalize the filing with pricing details, and begin roadshow plans. Ensure alignment with the chosen exchange, pricing, and roadshow strategy for a successful IPO.*

Zachary Blumenthal, Managing Director Investment Banking at Spartan Capital Securities LLC

When planning an IPO, finding a suitable investment bank and banking team, as well as preparing the S-1 draft, involves a thorough evaluation and selection process. Here are the key steps to consider:

- *Speak to your advisors (consultants, lawyers, accountants) about referrals to investment banks and their teams.*

- *Look at recent transactions for each referred bank to see what kind of transactions they do.*

- *Ask about the banks' pipeline and bandwidth to make sure your transaction will be treated with priority and care.*

When preparing the S-1 Draft:

- *Provide your lawyers with material items for a S-1 such as a description of the business, the cap table, executive and director compensation, issued warrants, convertible notes, options, and any other convertible or exercisable securities.*

- *Make sure your audit is complete as quickly as possible, that is generally the biggest gating factor for the filing of a S-1.*

- *Address comments and questions from advisors immediately to get the S-1 filed expediently with the SEC and Nasdaq/NYSE.*

CHAPTER 7 SUMMARY

- The investment banking team, and ultimately the right investment bank, is a key component in the micro-cap and small-cap IPO process.

- It is important to select an investment bank that focuses on micro-cap and small-cap investors. Investing in micro-cap, small-cap, mid-cap, or large-cap corresponds roughly to investors' risk and reward profiles.

- Make sure you take into account the bank's history with transactions, experience, and client successes, which will help you to identify the right individual banker.

- Choose a banker who will have a good rapport with management for the long term, including secondary offerings and capital market-related matters.

- You will also need to determine if the lead underwriter will be the sole book runner. Find out who will be responsible for coordinating and leading a well-organized underwriting syndicate.

- Ask your prospective bank about the banks it is likely to form a syndicate with, about its distribution capabilities, and about its distribution strategies.

- The investment bank you choose has a variety of purposes, including underwriting new stock issues, following on debt and equity financings, overseeing mergers and acquisitions, and advising clients on strategic capital market matters.

- Understand your company's metrics before engaging the bankers and do not rush this process.

- Compile a list of core comparison companies, look at these companies for comparable valuations, and identify similarities and differences.

- Prepare the S-1 draft, which is the business section of the SEC registration. It tells your company's story and contributes to the content of the pitch deck used for your investor roadshow.

- Finally, call a board meeting and present your case for the bank and banker you plan to choose for the IPO. Ask the board to take a vote.

CHAPTER 8
SHOW ME THE MONEY!

When approaching a micro-cap or small-cap IPO, getting to know your investors is sometimes overlooked entirely or left to the last days of the roadshow. Connecting directly with your investors, getting to know them, and educating them on your company story are integral parts of the IPO process. Doing so will go a long way toward success when you finally operate as a public company.

Micro-cap and small-cap investors operate within a community and often co-invest within the same network. Thus, knowing your investors will prove helpful in the future as your micro-cap or small-cap company matures and you need support for strategic initiatives in the future. Investors have different strategies. It is crucial to know who you are inviting to take ownership of your company during an IPO.

GETTING INVESTOR ATTENTION

One of the biggest challenges for a newly listed micro-cap or small-cap company is gaining investor attention to purchase shares in the IPO and in the open marketplace. Unfortunately, many micro-cap and small-cap companies do not prepare for investor awareness leading into the IPO. Nor do they have a plan to create visibility. This becomes especially difficult during the SEC-required quiet period, which starts when you publicly file your registration with the SEC.

Before going public, invest time in getting to know potential investors at various investment banks and industry conferences that offer companies a chance to present their businesses and hold one-on-ones with potential investors. These events are easy to find when you begin to talk to industry professionals who can recommend the conferences you should attend.

During the quiet period, regulation restricts companies from doing undue promotion that may influence or condition the market and affect the opening price of an IPO. That said, there are several ways to work with investors, even before you go public, to properly educate them on your story, and the plans you have for the future. First, companies may create a customary and consistent way of marketing and promotion, which may be continued during the quiet period.

It's best to create a media and awareness campaign at least a year before the IPO and set a high standard of customary marketing to the public. Unfortunately, most companies fail to create this program. Upon entering the quiet period, such companies realize the need for the public's attention only to find that the option is now closed.

WHO ARE THESE PEOPLE?

Your bankers will bring investors to the IPO and drive the distribution of IPO share allocations. You have a certain amount of influence on the allocations and a say in who gets to purchase your shares. Before pricing, it is essential to do your homework on the investors. Be sure you understand whom you want and don't want in the IPO.

Micro-cap and small-cap investors often have high churn rates and tend to look for structured financing with common shares and warrants. Focus on understanding the investors' investment strategies and goals, especially those who are oriented toward long-term holding periods.

Identify which investors may have high churn rates of selling their IPO shares early. You can conduct searches for high-quality investors globally by researching shareholders in your peer companies and tracking the size of their investments and churn portfolios. Churn rates give you some idea of how long investors may hold your shares. Then, you can map that information on the timeframe you have to achieve significant company milestones.

Global investors seek investments in your company's story and growth prospects. When it comes time to price your IPO, provide higher allocation to investors who express a longer hold period and give the company time to mature. Look for investors who are open and honest about their investment strategy. You'll recognize them as the ones who want to understand your company's story and vision for creating long-term value.

It's important to recognize that investors will come and go when you are a publicly traded company. Often the most challenging part of being a public company is dealing with the ongoing naysayers creating short sell opportunities for themselves with no basis in reality. However, over time, you can see trends in your shareholder base and better understand the activity in your shareholder base.

INVESTOR RELATIONSHIPS

Maintaining ongoing investor relationships creates a strong foundation as a public company. Communicate with your investors often and consistently to gain investor trust. This is accomplished by being open and honest with them about your wins and challenges. Update your investors regularly and stay directly connected to them as much as possible. This takes consistent work to cultivate but forms the basis of a great relationship when done correctly.

Consistently communicate the good news and, even more importantly, the bad news to strengthen investor relationships. Creating trust and goodwill with your investors will pay dividends in the future. Of course, the investors you want to obtain your stock should have a long-term view of your story. That story needs to manifest itself over the investment timelines of those investors.

INVESTOR VOLATILITY

Many micro-cap and small-cap investors represent themselves as long funds, which is where they will hold your IPO shares. However, many of these same funds also maintain a hedge fund operation with short holding periods and short positions. A short position occurs when investors sell shares of your stock that they do not own. Investors who sell short believe the price of the stock will decrease in value. If the price drops, they can buy the stock at a lower price and make a profit. This is a common practice. This volatility is part of the dynamic of becoming a publicly traded micro-cap or small-cap company.

After your IPO, trading volatility can be expected because your company has a limited number of shares in the market to fight off market manipulation. You can battle the volatility (to a degree) by working hard with your good investors to ensure that they understand the company's real story, growth strategies, and performance.

Unfortunately, very few micro-cap and small-cap IPO investors will hold your stock long-term. So, it's worth learning to accept and embrace the volatility of being a micro-cap or small-cap public company as a part of the world you will live in post-IPO.

Developing investor relations continues to be a strategically important function that signals market trust and confidence. IPO-bound companies that have established investor relations function well before their IPO and infix trust and confidence in that market. In turn, capital markets are more likely to reward the company with a higher valuation when its leader rings the bell and functions as a public company.

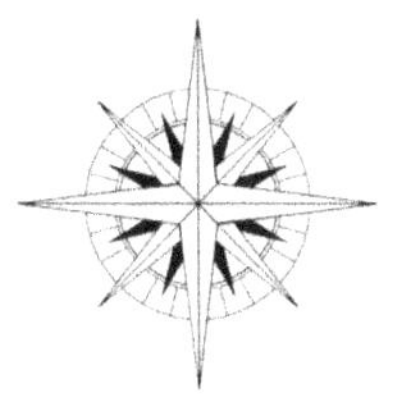

Tips from the Pros

Erik Sloan, Chief Revenue Officer at NEO Exchange

- *The first step when seeking investors is to start when your idea has taken shape and your business plan is robust.*

- *Investors are more likely to show interest when they see a clear vision, a well-defined market opportunity, and a solid execution strategy. Take the time to refine your pitch, ensuring that it effectively communicates the value proposition and growth potential of your venture.*

- *Developing strong investor relationships is crucial. It goes beyond simply presenting your business concept; it involves showcasing your passion, expertise, and dedication to achieving your goals. Investors not only want to invest in a promising venture but also in the people behind it. Take the opportunity to highlight your team's strengths, past accomplishments, and their alignment with the business objectives.*

- *In the investment community, it's crucial to be aware of the prevailing trends and preferences. Stay up to date with the latest developments in your industry and understand the investment landscape. Research potential investors to identify those who have a track record of investing in businesses similar to yours or have a particular interest in your sector. Seek out forums, events, and networks where you can connect with investors and learn from their experiences.*

- *While pursuing investor attention, be mindful of the alignment between your values and those of the investment community. Seek investors who share your vision and values, as they are more likely to provide the necessary support and guidance beyond financial backing. Consider factors such as their investment thesis, their focus on social or environmental impact, and their approach to risk management. Building a strong partnership with investors who share your values can lead to long-term success and positive impact.*

Elliot Milian, Managing Partner at Hybrid Financial Limited

How to get investor attention:

When planning an IPO, getting investor attention and developing investor relationships are essential for a successful offering. Here are some strategies to consider:

- *You should be using digital marketing, social media, forums, etc. There is an endless sea of opportunities and ways to speak to this community. Maintain an informative and up-to-date investor relations website that provides access to key information, financial reports, presentations, and news updates. Leverage social media platforms to share relevant company news, thought leadership, and industry insights.*

- *As for when to start ... YESTERDAY! In other words, as soon as possible.*

- *In order to develop investor relationships, education is king. Respect their time and always do as you say and say as you do. If you tell someone you will send something do it. Every detail matters when you are fighting against 5000 other companies and your peers.*

CHAPTER 8 SUMMARY

- Don't wait to get to know your investors until the roadshow.

- Gaining investor attention in order to purchase shares in the IPO and marketplace will be a challenge.

- Having a plan for investor awareness leading up to the IPO will avert difficulties during the SEC-required quiet period.

- The quiet period restricts companies from doing undue promotion that may influence or condition the market and affect the opening price of an IPO.

- Create a customary and consistent way of marketing and promotion.

- Start a media and awareness campaign at least a year before the IPO and set a high standard of customary marketing to the public.

- Focus on understanding the investors' investment strategies and goals, especially those who are oriented toward long-term holding periods.

- Provide higher allocation to investors who express a longer hold period and give the company time to mature. Look for investors who are open and honest about their investment strategy.

- **Maintain ongoing investor relationships to create a strong foundation as a public company. Communicate with your investors often and consistently to gain investor trust by being open and honest with them about your wins and challenges.**

- **Remember that trading volatility can be expected after your IPO because your company has a limited number of shares in the market to fight off market manipulation. You can battle the volatility (to a degree) by working hard with your good investors to ensure that they understand the company's real story, growth strategies, and performance.**

CHAPTER 9
ARE YOU REALLY READY?

IPO readiness for micro-cap and small-cap companies is a complex process. The time and resources required to prepare fully are often overlooked, understaffed, and underestimated. The good news is that it doesn't have to be this way.

During the current market turbulence we're experiencing, companies that are considering an IPO need to start their preparation as early as possible in order to capitalize on opportunity windows that present themselves later. For companies that missed out on IPO activity during 2022 and 2023, there is still positive news. When the IPO market resumes, the companies that are well prepared, after having spent this latest period focusing on IPO readiness, will be ready to list successfully.

Preparing for an IPO generally requires a minimum of six months and as much as twenty-four months of preparation before listing. Companies that are considering an IPO in the next two years must remember that *starting early is key*. Smart management teams will take advantage of this lull in the market to plan.

During this time, in addition to organizing the business and a team for a public offering, it is critically important to focus on your business performance. You'll also want to continue communicating to the investment community how you are executing your business model. You will also want to stay keenly focused on your short, mid, and long term goals.

PLANNING TO GO PUBLIC IN THE FUTURE?

IPO readiness is an essential step in the IPO process. It helps to ensure that the company is fully prepared to go public and that it can secure the best possible terms and valuation when it does so. Traditional IPO readiness means that the company has solid systems, controls, financial reporting, and governance structures in place. It means that the company is fully compliant with SEC regulations and that it can effectively communicate its story to potential investors.

The areas I like to focus on, which go way beyond traditional readiness, include strategic messaging, creating an IR strategy for retail, institutional investor awareness, and meeting with prospective investors, equity research analysts, and stakeholders. Additionally, IPO readiness can help to minimize the risk of delays or complications during the IPO process, which can be costly and time-consuming. Readiness can also help increase the chances of the IPO's success, which is crucial for the company's long-term growth and success. Furthermore, going public can be costly, so companies need to have enough resources on hand and plan for their use accordingly. Without an IPO readiness plan, a company may face serious challenges. These include having to delay or even cancel IPO plans, which can be detrimental to a company's reputation and future opportunities.

Although IPO preparation is a crucial step in the journey, programs to help micro-cap and small-cap companies prepare are not available in this sector. For this reason, I have created an IPO readiness program, which is the first of its kind for micro-cap and small-cap companies that seek an IPO. The program is specifically designed to redefine the criteria, costs, timelines, and processes of listing on senior global stock exchanges and securing transformational capital.

THE FIVE PILLARS

To simplify the IPO readiness process, I have designed a readiness roadmap that is focused on the key elements you will need to have in place to realistically identify any gaps in your business and documentation. It will also identify any gaps in processes that need to be addressed before beginning the IPO process.

A thorough review of each foundational building block captured by the five pillars of IPO readiness is critical to successful IPO execution. Importantly, missing, sub-par, or incomplete constituent elements may need to be upgraded (or created if not already in existence) to present your business as being consistent with public market investor expectations. The five key elements of IPO readiness are summarized below.

1. **Business Readiness.** Business IPO readiness requires the coherent articulation of the core elements of the business, which will be unique to the company in question. Generally, it will encompass critical areas such as the business' strategy, markets, products, sales, marketing, operations, financial statements, and metrics.

2. **Diligence Readiness.** IPO due diligence preparation involves the organization, collection, and collating of a wide variety of documents reflective of all aspects of the business, including legal, insurance, environmental, regulatory filings, human

resource contracts, compensation, policies, and matters of intellectual property such as trademarks and patents.

3. **S-1 Readiness.** Preparing the S-1 registration statement involves the creation of a basic business description consistent with the SEC regulatory requirements. This involves a summarized explanation of the business, its customers, its competition, and other information relevant to investors who want to make an informed investment decision regarding the company and its prospects.

4. **Audit Readiness.** Footnotes and schedules are required when compiling the company's financial statements to ensure that the company's financial reporting complies with industry standards. The footnotes also provide reasonable assurance that the financial statements are presented fairly, free from material misstatement, and thus can be relied upon by investors.

5. **Organizational Readiness.** The assembly of a management team, advisors, and board, including the form and structure of management compensation, is critical. The management team, advisors, and board need to be optimally aligned with the company's strategic objectives and public market expectations, so that they can guide the company's operations successfully and provide public market reporting.

FIVE KEY DELIVERABLES

There are five sets of direct outcomes that are expected from preparing a comprehensive set of IPO readiness materials and capabilities.

1. **Business Deliverables**: a company deck, a one- or two-page teaser, and a comprehensive financial model

2. **Diligence Deliverables**: a well-organized and up-to-date data room populated with the standard due diligence documents and schedules required by IPO bankers, auditors, and lawyers

3. **S-1 Deliverables**: company sections of the SEC registration statement and Management Discussion and Analysis (MD&A) of the company's recent financial performance

4. **Audit Deliverables**: two years of profit and loss, balance sheet, cash-flow statements, related footnotes, and supporting schedules

5. **Organization Deliverables:** clearly defined leadership team, compensation, and incentive plans, including bonus, equity plans, methodologies, cap table, governance, and a well-structured board of directors

Although the broader IPO market is seemingly on pause due to less-than-ideal marketplace conditions, know that these market conditions are not here to stay, at least not forever. Companies that are considering an IPO would be wise to use the current pause period to hustle while they wait and prepare, prepare, then prepare some more to become IPO ready. Thorough preparation requires that your company not only takes the proper steps and does the right things but also invests in the right partners, resources, technology tools, and team.

Teams that prepare to take the company public by meeting milestones, and learning to run the company for the long run, will enjoy public market success. Being ready and well-prepared is a critically important step on the IPO journey.

Tips from the Pros

Brian Zucker, Partner at Rosenberg Rich Baker Berman and Company

I would argue that there are several benefits to getting ready for an IPO in advance of actually going public. Here's how I would do it:

- *Start the financial reporting/audit process as early as possible to avoid costly delays.*

- *Usually, 2 years of audited financial statements need to be presented in an IPO, but audits take time and must meet age requirements or they go "stale." If the time between the latest balance sheet presented and the date of the IPO filing is more than 134 days the financials are considered stale. This is something to keep in mind.*

- *There are common areas of complex accounting issues that can cause delays; debt and equity agreements, share-based compensation, revenue recognition, the fair value of financial instruments including derivatives, warrant liabilities, and embedded conversion features. Depending on the financial instruments issued by the company a valuation specialist may be needed.*

Bill Caragol, Chief Financial Officer at Mainz BioMed

Some key items to consider when preparing to IPO in advance:

- *Know what you need and what you already have – leverage an expert who has been there/ done that – both legal and financial – to lay out a project plan.*

- *Meet with at least three investment bankers and listen to the nuances of how they view your company, expect to position it in the market, and their most recent deals – what worked and what didn't work. This will help you determine if they are a good fit for you and your company.*

- *An IPO is a large project with a lot of moving parts, so you'll need to assign a project manager. This could be a CFO, General Counsel, or an external resource – but someone on your team needs to be on top of the project tasks every day.*

CHAPTER 9 SUMMARY

- Micro-cap or small-cap IPO readiness and preparation are complex processes that require a significant amount of time and resources.

- Companies that are considering an IPO should begin preparing *now* to capitalize on opportunity windows that will present themselves later.

- It is important for companies to focus on their business performance, organizational readiness, and communication with the investment community during the preparation period.

- IPO readiness will minimize the risk of delays or complications during the IPO process and increase the chances of success.

- The author's program for IPO readiness for micro-cap and small-cap companies includes Five Pillars.

- The Five Pillars are business readiness, diligence readiness, S-1 readiness, audit readiness, and organizational readiness.

- The program aims to redefine the criteria, costs, timelines, and processes of listing on senior global stock exchanges and securing transformational capital.

CHAPTER 10
IT'S SHOW TIME!

As a part of preparing for an IPO, you will have developed the investor messaging, business, and financial model, and completed the business section of your S-1. You will now need to create an IPO deck for your roadshow. This deck will then be reviewed by your lawyers, the underwriter, and their counsel.

THE IPO ROADSHOW DECK

The guidelines for the deck include a maximum twenty-minute pitch. This includes telling a compelling story about how your company, product, or service line came about as well as your team and your value proposition. In addition, you will need to present your business model and describe how it will benefit from the IPO. You will need to show a pathway for investor return on investment.

There's a basic rule of thumb for effective slide presentation: *Less is more*. So, use fewer, more impactful words. You'll want to consider other things when preparing your presentation. First, bigger is better (minimum font size of eighteen, twenty-four or larger preferred). Second, be visual. Use graphics to convey key data and/or concepts. Finally, go pro. Professional polishing is highly recommended.

Introduce your management team, what role each member plays, and how each member will contribute to the execution and growth of the company. Then, do dry runs with your team and the bankers to drill down on the nuances of the wording, the key messages, the timing, the effectiveness of examples, and the order of topics. Rehearse, get to the point, know your numbers, convey confidence, and then rehearse again.

The roadshow is a time-sensitive window before the IPO where many discussions on various topics will occur with the SEC, the exchange, and your bankers. During this time-sensitive window, the SEC will review your filing and provide comments and questions regarding your disclosures, your business, and the risk factors. The SEC will require complete disclosure of material information.

Simultaneously, the exchange will review your application, provide comments, and ask questions regarding your application. The exchange will determine if you are meeting the quantitative and qualitative listing requirements. During this time, you will continue to work closely with your advisors to sort out the proper responses in order to satisfy the SEC examiners. Then, the responses by the SEC examiners are critical to managing your timeline to IPO. The content you give to the SEC will be reviewed closely by third parties, and live forever in the document you file publicly.

TESTING THE WATERS

Testing the Waters (TTW) in the IPO process allows companies to gauge how successful investors receive their prospective IPO before committing to further time, expense, and scrutiny of a public offering of securities. This is especially true for an IPO by a company that is not already subject to public company reporting requirements.

The TTW of the capital markets allows for greater transparency and communication between the company and the investors, before the full-blown IPO process. It enables companies to adjust their strategy for the IPO. In addition, it allows investors to assess whether or not they want to invest. TTW periods are designed to help inform a management team and the underwriters about whether they should endeavor to raise capital from the public equity market before going through the actual process of going public.

The TTW roadshow allows management to meet with select investors to see how the opportunity is received and underwriters to gain an indication of interest. This process is valuable for management to see how investors react to you presenting and describing the business. In addition, you can gauge how the audience received the story. This allows prospective investors the opportunity to gain a significantly better understanding of the business. You get the opportunity to refine your message after every presentation.

ON THE ROAD AGAIN

The primary reason for the IPO roadshow is to allow companies to generate enough interest from investors to raise the capital necessary to go from a private firm to a public one. In addition, it enables listing companies to understand their standing in the market. If done successfully, IPO roadshows can create an oversupply of capital to help drive a company's long-term success, and accelerate its growth.

Scheduling and planning the roadshow has changed since the pandemic. Now it is primarily done virtually. However, depending on logistics and transportation, traveling for the roadshow is still an option. Based on experience, seven to ten days is adequate time to generate interest for orders to sell your issuance. On the other hand, if you are traveling to major financial centers in the U.S., you might want to extend this timeframe. Your job is to tell your story well and convey confidence. It is your stock to sell. While it is not absolutely necessary to travel to meet investors, the roadshow is an opportunity to meet your future major shareholders face-to-face and to make personal introductions.

Choose investors you can build a strong relationship with over time. After the IPO, you will need to work hard to develop and grow relationships with your key IPO investors and with new ones.

Be aware of the types of investors you meet with and do your research before the roadshow. The pace is break-neck and your bankers will cater to their best customers, that is, hedge funds and short sellers.

It is possible to view the micro-cap and small-cap industry as a game, that is to say, there is a level of com-petition and strategy involved in investing in micro-cap and small-cap companies. However, it is important to note that the micro-cap and small-cap industries involve real companies and real financial risks (and rewards), so it is not a game in the traditional sense.

It is important to approach investments in the micro-cap and small-cap industry with caution and a thorough under-standing of the risks involved. Of course, your bankers will want to make sure their best clients get an allocation. So, make sure you get to designate significant allocations to the investors you wish to deal with and, whenever possible, avoid the folks you don't want to deal with.

MANAGING THE CALENDAR

While management is out Testing the Waters, the finance and legal teams are busy updating the registration, addressing regulatory comments, clarifying statements, and providing further commentary in response to requests from the SEC and the exchange. The next milestone is to file your S-1 per your planned IPO date, and fine-tune the calendar of events. After that, your company must make its first public filing with the SEC at least fifteen days before it commences roadshows to market the offering. The purpose of this fifteen-day cooling off period is to let the market absorb the information regarding the issuer and the contemplated securities offering that has been under confidential review.

You will also be coordinating activities with your chosen exchange regularly. One of the tasks here will be to schedule your IPO's pricing and trading day. You will also want to get on the exchange's schedule to ring the opening bell. Timing is everything, so close contact and continued relationship-building with the exchange will help to set this up.

IPO day is one of the most exciting events for an entrepreneur. It will also be one of the biggest lead generation days you will ever have. Marketing takes time and resources to plan and create visibility. Hence, you develop a plan and a timeline to take full advantage of the publicity it generates.

Tips from the Pros

Ross Carmel, Founding Partner at Carmel, Milazzo & Feil LLP

Testing the Waters:

- *Testing the waters before you dive into a roadshow, allows you and the investment bank and* you to give your presentation to institutional investors before your registration statement is publicly available. These meetings give companies a chance to gauge and generate investor interest in a public offering prior to engaging in a formal roadshow. Basically, it allows for a company to evaluate the market, and for the market, in turn, to evaluate the company exploring an IPO before expending additional costs and resources. Further, any feedback received during the testing the waters process can be used to refine your presentation when going on the roadshow.

- Information in testing the waters communications cannot conflict with material information in the registration statement and the Company must avoid any material misstatements or omissions.

- Any written materials provided to investors should be collected at the end of the presentation, as potential investors should not be allowed to maintain any written materials.

IPO Roadshow deck:

- All information and facts set forth in the deck must also be disclosed in the S-1.

- The deck should be eye-catching, and tell the story of your Company clearly, accurately, and quickly. Focus on what sets your business apart, makes it special, and drives current and future value for your business and potential investors.

Going on the Road:

- *Be confident, be likable, be prepared, and tell your story with a clear vision of the future.*

- *Be confident. There is a reason you are in a position to go public, as you have built a successful business, so act like it. This is your opportunity to convince investors to participate in your offering, so be confident about your business, its model, and your vision to grow the business.*

- *Be likeable. You are telling a story, and like any sale, people tend to invest or buy from people they like. A likeable management team, who are passionate about their business, can be the difference between an investor choosing to or not to invest in your offering.*

- *Be prepared. Practice makes perfect, and you should have your pitch memorized before going on the roadshow and refine your story to make it clear and easy to understand. You need to know every in and out of your business, your competitors, vision for the future, with a clear expression of how you get there. You should anticipate the questions an investor will ask and incorporate them into your pitch.*

Andrew Tucker, Partner at Nelson Mullins Riley & Scarborough

Testing the Waters and the Roadshow is an important time in the IPO process. Here's what you should know:

- *The roadshow deck becomes a publicly filed document since it will likely be the free-writing prospectus so don't make statements you can't back up. You'll want to treat the deck like a prospectus in terms of diligence and attention because many investors will only read this in place of the prospectus, so be certain that the company highlights are included.*

- *During the Testing the Waters period, make sure that you take the feedback seriously. If the feedback is negative, stay focused and consider how to best move forward. Remember that every dollar you give up in valuation now is a dollar you have to earn back. However, it is better to leave some money on the table so you have happy investors than take every last penny and have sad investors.*

- *When going on the road, remember that you know the company through and through, so make sure you also know the presentation through and through. I always recommend that you try to get someone from the outside to listen to the presentation before you finalize it, someone with some familiarity with the business but not someone who is too close to the document. And finally, companies frequently want to take shortcuts and make assumptions during this process. This is not something you want to come through in the roadshow, the presentation, or testing the waters. Take the time, and do not cut corners.*

CHAPTER 10 SUMMARY

- Prepare an IPO deck for your roadshow. This will need to be reviewed by your lawyers, the underwriter, and their counsel.

- The guidelines for the deck include a maximum twenty-minute pitch, including a compelling story about your company, product or service line, your team, and your value proposition.

- Present your business model and how it will benefit from the IPO. Show a pathway for investor return on investment.

- Use fewer, more impactful words and large font with visuals to convey key data and concepts.

- Introduce your management team and the role of each team member. Do dry runs with your team and the bankers to drill down on wording, key messages, timing, and order of topics.

- Rehearse, know your numbers, convey confidence, and rehearse again.

- The roadshow is a time-sensitive window before the IPO where many discussions will occur with the SEC, the exchange, and your bankers.

- Simultaneously, the SEC will review your filing and provide comments and questions regarding your disclosures, business, risk factors, and material information.

- Testing the Waters (TTW) in the IPO process allows companies to gauge how successful investors receive their prospective IPO before committing to further time, expense, and scrutiny of a public offering of securities.

- TTW periods are designed to help inform a management team and the underwriters on whether they should start raising capital from the public equity market before initiating the actual process of going public.

- The TTW roadshow allows management to meet with select investors to see how the opportunity is received and underwriters to gain an indication of interest.

- This process is valuable for management to see how investors react to you presenting and describing the business.

- The primary reason for the IPO roadshow is to allow companies to generate enough interest from investors to raise the capital necessary to go from a private to a public firm.

CHAPTER 11
YOU'VE ARRIVED!

The IPO Listing Day is a milestone event that many entrepreneurs have looked forward to for many years. All the hard work that led you to this day, the months or years of preparation, the final weeks with bankers and investors, and the countless hours with the legal and financial teams all culminate in this memorable day in your company's history.

The day shares open for trading on the markets is called the Listing Day and a lot happens on this day behind the scenes. The opening bell signals the start of trading for the stock market and the exchange your shares are listed on. On this day, your company transforms into a publicly traded entity and starts a new phase in its corporate history.

The mechanics of pricing your stock, final due diligence, and shares allotted based on investor interest will be completed the night before the exchange listing. Your underwriter will match up investor demand and interest to set the offering price and, in conjunction with the exchange and legal teams, will also go through a process to support the initial trading on Listing Day. Investors will receive their allotment of shares, coordinated by the underwriter, the transfer agent, and company counsel before the market opens. Then, the investors officially become shareholders and shares are ready to become formally listed on the stock market.

Pricing and execution of the mechanics of Listing vary between the exchanges. But the result of the company's stock opening for trading and the stock's continuous trading is the same. Upon the stock trading, the IPO investors are now free to sell their shares in the open market, which is also known as the secondary market. As a result, the day of your IPO is memorable but frenetic.

For many entrepreneurs doing this for the first time, it is one of their careers' more intense yet satisfying journeys. Completing your IPO is a time to celebrate, reflect, and enjoy. The rigorous process it took to get you and your team to this moment will be some of the most challenging to experience. Therefore, making it to Listing Day is a momentous occasion.

PLANNING FOR LISTING DAY

During the 2020 Pandemic, the initial Listing Day and bell-ringing ceremonies changed in an effort to curb close contact and adhere to COVID-19 safety standards. Before the COVID-19 pandemic, the exchange would have an IPO ceremony where executives, employees, and family members from the company came to the exchange to celebrate the IPO at the opening bell.

During this time, the exchanges shifted to virtual IPOs and remote first trades to enable companies to facilitate their initial public offerings in a safe and healthy environment. Companies could celebrate with a virtual bell ringing and have scheduled celebrations to ring the NASDAQ or NYSE opening or closing bell in person after an IPO.

Now that we are post-pandemic, in-person bell-ringing ceremonies have returned. Companies, once again, have the once-in-a-lifetime experience of ringing the opening or closing bell at their chosen exchange.

Wherever you are situated, your first IPO day is meant to be celebrated and organized for all the company employees, shareholders, and stakeholders as a special and historic once-in-a-lifetime event. Whatever way you wish to celebrate this new beginning, it requires planning and coordination to memorialize the IPO and commence the next great adventure of being a publicly listed company.

GOING TO MARKET

While the markets open at 9:30 a.m., your company's trading may not occur at the opening bell, as most new listings of an IPO separate these special events away from the markets' official 9:30 a.m. opening for continuous trading to occur between 10:00 a.m. and 3:00 p.m. You may become glued to the trading panel where you can see the price movements in your stock and the first trade. Seeing your stock ticker on the screen for the first time is a momentous experience.

The value that the investors paid for the shares may be different from the target price given in the IPO prospectus as determined by the underwriters and your company. If there was a lot of interest in the shares and your company pre-IPO, the opening stock price might be higher than in the prospectus. Once trading commences, you will see the stock ticker and price movement. And whether it is up, down, back up, or back down, it is a crazy yet exhilarating day.

TRADING VOLATILITY

Micro-cap and small-cap stocks tend to have greater volatility. That is why they are inherently riskier than large-cap stocks. After you complete your IPO, be prepared for the stock price to fluctuate as investors buy and sell the shares. Also, trading in your company's stock is likely to be highly volatile for the first several months upon listing. This is entirely normal and to be expected. There is often limited information on newly listed micro-cap and small-cap companies and it takes less volume to move prices upwards and downwards. Going public is turbulent under the best of times. After the record-breaking IPO year of 2021, things have been markedly more complex and volatile in 2022 and 2023, amid inflationary concerns and a challenging global geopolitical environment.

In addition, newly listed micro-cap and small-cap companies have been under increased scrutiny by regulators and exchanges due to market manipulation of micro-cap and small-cap stocks, which resulted in more volatility. A reality of being a public company is that many investors short a stock as a trading strategy and expect the value of the stock to go down. While there are regulatory and practical obstacles to short selling IPO shares, any stock can be shorted, even with limitations set by underwriters. This includes short selling company stock on the day of its IPO by institutional investors who have purchased the stock and lent it out for short selling.

THE REALITY OF SHORT SELLING

Short selling is risky because, theoretically, the loss on a short trade can be infinite since a stock price can go as high as there are numbers. The SEC has recently proposed new rules that require some investors to report their short-sale related activity to the SEC monthly. This allows the SEC to make detailed short selling data available to the public for the first time. It will take time for the market and the regulatory environment to improve in a way that makes the IPO market less volatile. As a result, companies will be best served by focusing on delivering solid performance. Once market conditions improve, uncertainty would be removed from the market. As sentiment from institutional investors improves, more investors and capital will enter the market. During this time of market turbulence, it is crucial to focus on your business performance, and to communicate to the investment community how you are executing your business model and how you are staying focused on your short, mid, and long term goals.

For investors currently missing out on IPO activity, there's good news. When the IPO market resumes, the companies that have gone public or will IPO in the future have better foundations after spending this latest period focusing on fundamental issues like profitability, cash flow, and expense management.

Tips from the Pros

Jay Heller, Head of Capital Markets at Nasdaq Inc.

- *Whether a start-up that is interested in learning more about the IPO process or a late-stage company already down the path of going public, creating an IPO and listing-day check-list is essential. These steps and key learnings are based on Nasdaq's 52-year track record of helping thousands of companies successfully transition to public markets.*

- *Getting started: Identify counsel and auditors, while also taking time to determine roles and responsibilities for the complete list of matters pertaining to an IPO. This is also the time to identify prospective investment bankers and analysts, and select the stock exchange the company intends to list on and ensure the company will meet the applicable listing standards.*

- *Understand the Process: Nasdaq's IPO process was built in collaboration with the investment banking community. Nasdaq leverages data and technology, while providing a world-class execution team to have a flawless IPO and open stocks at the most optimal price.*

- *Stay in the Moment: IPO day is a momentous occasion in a company's lifecycle. Nasdaq is proud to welcome brands of all shapes and sizes from around the world, utilizing its state-of-the-art approach to ensure all companies have an unparalleled listing experience on "day-one". It is important to remember that listing day is a marathon and not a sprint. Above all, enjoy the day knowing that your exchange of choice is supporting the future and evolution of your company.*

Paul Dorfman, Head of Listings, NYSE American

- *On Listing Day, your company's leadership team should be well-prepared and public-company ready. Specifically:*

- *Be ready to discuss the company's narrative and value proposition within the bounds of your public disclosures.*

- *Don't let the high level of excitement you will feel on this day prompt you to step beyond your prepared messaging.*

- *Understand that as a public company, you will face a new level of scrutiny around your actions and performance.*

- *Enjoy the moment! Take a picture of your team at the New York Stock Exchange so you can look back on what you've accomplished.*

CHAPTER 11 SUMMARY

- The IPO Listing Day is a milestone event that marks the end of months or years of preparation and the beginning of a new phase for the company as a publicly traded entity.

- On this day, the opening bell signals the start of trading for the stock market and investors officially become shareholders.

- The night before the exchange listing, the mechanics of pricing the stock, final due diligence, and shares allotted based on investor interest will be completed.

- The underwriter will match up investor demand and interest to set the offering price and support the initial trading on Listing Day.

- Investors will receive their allotment of shares, coordinated by the underwriter, the transfer agent, and company counsel before the market opens.

- The stock's continuous trading is the same and, upon trading, the IPO investors are now free to sell their shares in the open market.

- The day of the IPO is memorable, frenetic and a time to celebrate, reflect, and enjoy.

- **Due to the pandemic, the exchanges have shifted to virtual IPOs and remote first trades. Companies celebrate with a virtual bell ringing.**

- **IPO day should be organized and celebrated for all the company employees, shareholders, and stakeholders.**

- **The markets open at 9:30 a.m. but the company's trading may not occur at the opening bell. Instead, it may occur between 10:00 a.m. and 3:00 p.m.**

- **The value that the investors paid for the shares may be different from the target price given in the IPO prospectus. The open price might be higher than in the prospectus if there was a lot of interest in the shares pre-IPO.**

- **Once trading commences, the stock ticker and price movement will be visible.**

CHAPTER 12
IT'S OFFICIAL. NOW WHAT?

You've celebrated your IPO. But now the long game of being a sustainable public company begins. While this significant accomplishment is often a life-changing event for most entrepreneurs, now the work of being public begins. And, at the same time, you still have the day-to-day operations of your business to run. It is a huge milestone to finally IPO and begin trading as a public company. However, now you must shift your focus to the long game and the measures of success that investors and Wall Street will be looking for from your business.

Many micro-cap and small-cap companies that go public are led by founders or CEOs who are new to the capital markets and are passionate visionaries. The good news is that you have completed your IPO, you are well-capitalized, and you can build on what made you successful before trading as a public company.

YOU'RE PUBLIC!

Going public is an opportunity to build on the success you've already created. It requires adjustments to manage the new challenges associated with public company growth and public company leadership. Now you will begin to see the benefits of the preparation and the systems you worked hard to implement before the IPO. The primary task right now is to set and communicate performance expectations to investors, so as to position the company for success to meet or exceed those expectations.

Once things settle down from your IPO and listing activities, refocus your management team and your employees on fundamentals of revenue, earnings, and cash flow. This will deliver a successful initial public quarter. Take care of the fundamentals and the business matters within your control. You'll notice that the IPO volatility and stock price will eventually settle down. Do your best not to keep looking at the stock ticker and worrying about the fluctuations.

GET PRACTICAL

Surround yourself with talented people who have experience running a public company. If you have gaps in your management team, it is not too late to hire top talent who understand the micro-cap and small-cap publicly traded environment. It's also essential to engage your board of directors in helping to understand and shape the future of your business and company culture, so it can support the growth and evolution of the company and the executive leadership.

Also, be sure to continue building internal and external communications for the varying stakeholders of the company. Be sure that you hone the messages and script to communicate to investors, analysts, media, and others consistently and effectively post-IPO.

MANAGING A PUBLIC COMPANY

With many new demands being placed on the executive team, it is critical to stay focused on key deliverables after the IPO. The market can reward your efforts or punish you depending on how you manage the business performance. The company's value is based on how well you manage the business, your customers, and your employees as well as how well you continue to communicate with stakeholders. Forecasting is especially important after the IPO to properly position the business for top performance and to set future expectations.

Investors focus on the operating cash flow as an indicator of the strength of your business model, your efforts to achieve profitability, and whether you will need to raise more funds and possibly dilute their interest in the company. Your company can no longer operate as it did when it was private. You must manage your team and workforce to deliver on crucial metrics daily. You will also need to make sure everyone is aware of the impact actions can have on the company's valuation. This will require you to hold people accountable for results.

There is no time to waste over issues to be addressed in the future. Your best practices in managing the business include addressing weaknesses quickly with short, mid and long term solutions. A critical part of any business and the forecasting process is understanding your cash flow. Especially in the current market, one of the key valuation metrics, next to revenue, is becoming cash-flow positive.

EDUCATING CURRENT AND FUTURE STAKEHOLDERS

Invest in investor education that focuses on educating and providing information to individuals who participate, or are considering participating, as investors in your company and sector within the financial markets. This will help investors better assess the opportunity of being a stakeholder. It is crucial to educate the investors on an ongoing basis to understand the risk vs. return better and promote long-term investment in your company.

The profile of your investors will change and be fluid along with the liquidity of your stock. But remember that the investors and analysts represent more than just money. They are also people. Therefore, building relationships with each of them is crucial.

Take advantage of all the information you can glean from your listing exchange and other financial services to understand who your current investors are and how they approach investing. Constantly assess how investors view your business. Ensure them that you address their concerns and manage their perceptions in press releases, earnings calls, and presentations.

Investors may become very knowledgeable about your business and industry, and see the trends, even if the company's business model takes an unexpected turn. It's still better to educate your investors than for them to be surprised with either good or bad information.

Don't miss forecasted numbers. It will take time to overcome that miss and could damage your credibility. However, you must predict and stay on top of the business results. So, create a skilled forecast team. Ensure that members of this team have the tools they need to do their job. Remember to communicate and educate investors on your performance.

MANAGING SEC REPORTING

To hold public companies accountable and create a transparent and fair market environment for investors, the SEC requires disclosing items related to a company's financial condition, operating results, management compensation, and other material events. Public company disclosures required by the SEC are lengthy and not limited to financial statements. Getting the reporting right involves discipline around reporting. This includes knowing what to disclose, when to disclose it, and the mechanics behind those disclosures.

Time seems to move very fast nowadays and seemingly even faster when you are a public company, as the days, weeks, months, and quarter-end seem to accelerate. Newly listed micro-cap and small-cap companies often struggle to comply with SEC reporting. Most companies take longer than the allotted time to release earnings and file quarterly and annual reports. The CEO and CFO are responsible for the quantity and accuracy of reporting required by the SEC, along with deadlines and disclosures for corporate transparency.

Remember that, once public, you cannot pick and choose what you want to share. Both good and bad material must be disclosed. Start the preparation of your financial reporting early. Make sure you are consistent with your corporate house cleaning and administrative matters. It is a best practice to track the latest SEC reviews of your benchmark companies. Search for insight into any new changes that might impact your business. And keep up to date on future accounting changes. Enjoy the ride and the benefits of playing the long game. You've worked hard to get here.

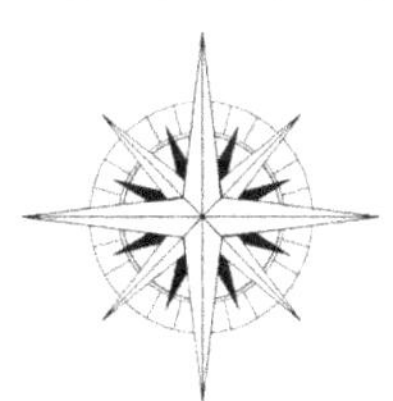

Tips from the Pros

Marc Seelenfreund, CEO of Siyata Mobile Inc.

In my experience, once a company has gone public, it is essential to focus on maintaining the sustainability and success of the newly established public company. Here are some key considerations for preparing the company for sustainability:

- *Make sure you have a solid Board of Directors including the various positions filled such as audit committee, comp committee etc. Boards of public companies have fiduciary responsibilities that you may not have as a private company so it's extremely important to have this in place.*

- *The lawyer used for your private company is probably not an SEC lawyer and it is key to have a very competent SEC legal team to work with as a public company. Get recommendations, spend time interviewing firms, negotiate terms, and don't necessarily go to a big-name firm. I've found it's often the smaller firms that will give you better service. Similarly, it is key to have a good auditor that knows the company, has a good working relationship, and will be the right firm to work with as the company grows.*

- *Finally, it's very important to have a good investor relations firm to work with because this can dramatically affect the stock price and volume. There are thousands of IR firms that all sell a very similar product and it's very hard to weed out the gems. Thus, it's important to get references, assure the personalities on your file are a good fit, and negotiate pricing.*

Vlado Bosanac, Founder & Head of Strategy at Advanced Health Intelligence

By focusing on shareholder education, effective SEC reporting, and sustainable governance practices, a company can position itself for long-term success as a public company while maintaining transparency, compliance, and shareholder confidence.

- *Preparing your company to become a sustainable public company requires a long-term perspective integrating environmental, social, and governance considerations into business strategy. This involves creating a culture of transparency, accountability, and responsible decision-making, and engaging stakeholders to build trust and support for your company's sustainability goals.*

- *As a public company, it is important to continue educating your shareholders about your sustainability performance and how it aligns with your business strategy. This requires clear and concise SEC reporting that highlights your progress and challenges and proactive engagement with shareholders to address their concerns and feedback.*

CHAPTER 12 SUMMARY

- The long game of being a sustainable public company begins after an IPO.

- The work of being public begins while you're still having to run the day-to-day operations of your business.

- Now the focus shifts to the long game and the measures of success that investors and Wall Street will be looking for from your business.

- Set and communicate performance expectations to investors and position the company for success to meet or exceed those expectations.

- Once things settle down from your IPO and listing activities, refocus your management team and your employees on the fundamentals of revenue, earnings, cash flow, and delivering a successful initial public quarter.

- Surround yourself with talented people who have experience running a public company.

- Engage your board of directors in helping to understand and shape the future of your business and company culture.

- Forecasting is especially important after the IPO to properly position the business for top performance and to set future expectations.

- **Investors focus on the operating cash flow as an indicator of the strength of your business model, your efforts to achieve profitability, and whether you will need to raise more funds and possibly dilute their interest in the company.**

- **The company can no longer operate as it did when it was private, so manage your team and workforce to deliver on crucial metrics daily.**

CONCLUSION

Congratulations on completing this compre-hensive roadmap for navigating the complex and dynamic world of IPOs. I want to thank you for your time and attention and commend your interest in learning and growing as an entrepreneur.

By delving into the various chapters and understanding the outlined strategies, you will have gained valuable and practical insights into the process of taking your company public. I hope that the knowledge you have gained from this book will be instrumental in your future endeavors. I truly believe that the steps highlighted throughout this book will provide you with a roadmap that can increase your chances of a successful IPO.

My goal for writing this book was to educate you on the numerous advantages an IPO can provide for micro-cap and small-cap companies, which include accessing capital, enhancing brand recognition, attracting potential investors, and creating liquidity for existing shareholders. However, embarking on this journey requires careful analysis, preparation, and execution. In Chapter 2, you learned the importance of thoroughly analyzing your company's readiness for an IPO. Assessing financial stability, growth potential, and market conditions will help determine the optimal time to go public.

Chapter 3 guided you in developing a strategic IPO roadmap and Chapter 4 discussed assembling the right team, including the board of directors, finance and legal teams, and other key individuals. Chapter 5 emphasized the significance of pre-IPO communications and awareness. By effectively marketing your company, engaging with investors, and preparing comprehensive documentation, you can generate interest and build anticipation for your IPO. Additionally, Chapter 6 highlighted the critical role of governance and selecting suitable board members who can contribute to the success of your public company.

Finding the right investment bank and banking team was discussed in Chapter 7, as they play a pivotal role in guiding you through the IPO process and helping you prepare the S-1 draft. Chapter 8 provided valuable insights on attracting investors, developing relationships, and navigating the investment community successfully.

Ensuring IPO readiness, as explored in Chapter 9, is vital for a smooth transition to being a publicly traded company. Adhering to the Exchange Listing IPO readiness program will help you meet regulatory requirements and establish credibility with shareholders. Chapter 10 covered the essential aspects of the IPO roadshow, including developing a compelling presentation deck, testing the waters, and conducting successful investor meetings.

On IPO day, as discussed in Chapter 11, you must plan for various logistics, such as the bell-ringing ceremony and market volatility. Managing trading volatility and addressing potential challenges like short sellers require a well-prepared and resilient approach. Lastly, in Chapter 12, you learned the importance of preparing your company for its new status as a public entity, educating shareholders, and managing SEC reporting effectively.

It is important to remember that the IPO process can be complex and demanding, requiring careful consideration and dedicated effort. Seek professional expertise, stay informed about evolving market trends, and adapt your strategies accordingly during the long journey, from the initial stages of building a company to the decision to go public.

An IPO is a pinnacle event for any entrepreneur and yet it is not an end in itself. Rather, it is a means to achieving broader business objectives, and so it will require perseverance, adaptability, and commitment. If you embark on this journey, I encourage you to stay true to your company's mission, vision, and values throughout the IPO process, which will resonate with investors and stakeholders in the long run.

You may be asking yourself, "What's next?" Suppose you're interested in delving deeper into the IPO process and feel your company may be ready for the public markets. In that case, my company, Exchange Listing, has developed a comprehensive IPO readiness roadmap. In this program, we redefine the criteria, costs, timelines, and listing processes on senior global stock exchanges and assist with securing transformational capital. Our execution model contains ten modules that explore five core pillars that we believe are the foundational building blocks for successful IPO execution.

I encourage you to apply the knowledge acquired, take bold steps toward your IPO journey, and make a positive impact through your entrepreneurial pursuits. If you're ready for the next step, which I hope you are, go to www.exchangelistingllc.com, connect with me on LinkedIn at https://www.linkedin.com/in/peter-goldstein-exchangelisting, and please consider me a resource in your journey.

ABOUT THE AUTHOR

Peter Goldstein is a seasoned entrepreneur and capital market expert with over 35 years of experience. His diverse background in international business has equipped him with valuable insights across various markets and industries.

Throughout his career, Peter has held key roles such as Founder investment banker, CEO, chairman, Board Member, Investor, and advisor to public, private, and emerging growth companies. He has achieved remarkable success in capital markets, leveraging his expertise in strategic planning, Financing, and transaction structuring. Peter has led and completed numerous IPOs, uplisting and, M&A, reverse merger transactions, private placements, and crowdfunding campaigns.

Peter began his entrepreneurial journey as the Founder and CEO of a specialty food distributor, pioneering the farm-to-table organic produce industry in renowned New York City restaurants.

Now, as the founder of Exchange Listing, LLC, Peter passionately provides growth companies with comprehensive strategic planning and implementation services to facilitate listings on esteemed exchanges like NASDAQ, NYSE, and NEO.

He is also the Founder and Managing Director of Emmis Capital, a specialized boutique fund, investing in global small-microcap pre-IPO growth companies, and serves as the CEO of Grandview Capital Partners, Inc., where he offers financial, operational, and organizational management and consulting services to businesses across the globe.He is also the Founder and Managing Director of Emmis Capital, a specialized fund, and serves as the CEO of Grandview Capital Partners, Inc., where he offers M&A, financial, operational, and organizational consulting services to businesses across the globe.

He also co-founded and chaired the board of Staffing 360 Solutions, Inc. (NASDAQ: STAF), a publicly traded company in the international staffing sector focused on acquiring domestic and international staffing agencies.

Holding an Advanced Corporate Directors certificate from Harvard Business School and an MBA in International Business from the University of Miami, Peter Goldstein is a highly accomplished professional. He has also held several FINRA registrations, including Series 7, 24, 79, 99, and 66.